Number Two

Number Two

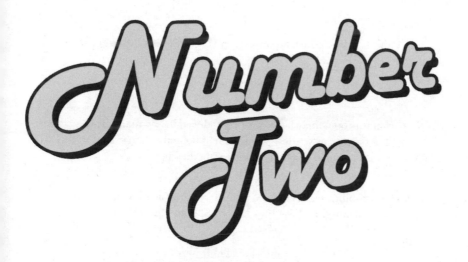

More Short Tales
from a Very Tall Man

JAY ONRAIT

Collins

Published by Collins, an imprint of HarperCollins Publishers Ltd

First edition

HarperCollins books may be purchased for educational, business,
or sales promotional use through our Special Markets Department.

HarperCollins Publishers Ltd
2 Bloor Street East, 20th Floor
Toronto, Ontario, Canada
M4W 1A8

www.harpercollins.ca

Library and Archives Canada Cataloguing in Publication
information is available upon request

ISBN 978-1-44343-494-2 (original trade paperback)

ISBN 978-1-44343-493-5 (hardcover)

Printed and bound in the United States of America
RRD 9 8 7 6 5 4 3 2 1

For Chobi

Number Two

Contents

Foreword

PETER SCHRAGER, SENIOR WRITER, FOXSPORTS.COM

So, we're sitting there.

The four of us.

First, there's Dan O'Toole, a disturbingly bloated 5-foot-something man with silver hair who'd betrayed his usual P90X workout regiment so cruelly over the previous three weeks that he now resembled—both in colour and shape—a Rubik's Cube far more than a (somewhat) adjusted father of two.

Next to inflated, red-faced Dan is Robert Lusetich, a 40-some-thing-year-old Aussie golf writer who reminds us throughout our trip that when he was a younger man living in Los Angeles, he was the star entertainment reporter for a Sydney-based daily newspaper. Robert has an eleven-minute "juicy" story for just about every celebrity you could name (as long as said celebrity walked a red carpet and/or spoke with him at a press junket between the years 1993 and 1999), and he loves to share these tales with anyone who'll give him the time to do so. Want a good Calista Flockhart yarn? Robert's got a few.

Although it would have been hard to imagine had you seen just *how* rose-coloured Dan's cheeks were at this point, Robert is somehow even more bloated and oozing more toxins than his Canadian tablemate.

I'm across from these two gentlemen, and I'm an unsettling mix of exhausted, uneasy, and uncertain.

Jay Onrait is seated next to me.

Tall. Wormlike. *So* Western Canadian. Jay's wearing some ironic T-shirt—a hipster band from Alberta, perhaps? A famous saying from the *Corner Gas* television show?—that I don't quite get. I'm on tilt and nervous, but Jay's just smiling ear to ear, having the time of his life.

"This is great, isn't it, fellas? All of us, here like this, with our lives potentially hanging in the balance? It's how it was meant to be. Really, it is. It's like we're in a Bond film. Hope it all works out for us, eh?!"

We're on the outskirts of Sochi, Russia (yes, you read that correctly—the Sochi *outskirts*), in a restaurant full of locals. It's our twenty-sixth and last day together in this foreign land, having spent the previous three and a half weeks covering the 2014 Winter Olympics for Fox Sports. It's also our first time "off" the Fox compound or outside the heavily secured Olympic Village. It's broad daylight in a crowded bar, and yet, I'm shaking nervously.

And that's because we've got company.

And not the good kind.

Four men. Seated at a table right next to us, not just smoking, but aggressively sucking the life out of their respective cigarettes like it was a contest to see who could inhale *more* smoke *harder*. They're staring—angrily—at the only four non-Russians in the place . . . us.

No words are exchanged with the men, but it's more than merely uncomfortable. It's unnerving. They don't smile, and they don't avert their eyes.

After months and months of being warned of potential danger overseas, I'm just twelve hours away from getting on a flight and being back, safe and sound, in my New York City apartment. All I wanted was lunch. And yet, we *had* to go somewhere "authentic." Somewhere "in town." We needed to see the *real* Sochi.

Now, these four men at the table next to us are mumbling to each other in a language we don't know and glaring at the four of *us* in an unfriendly way.

Dan and Robert are with me on this. We need to leave. As soon as possible. "Let's get the cheque and get out of here," I say with more than a subtle hint of urgency.

But Jay isn't having it.

"Oh, come on. They're probably just into your meal, Schrags. What'd you get? Is that borscht? They probably think your borscht looks good."

I look at my plate. Whatever I'd ordered (it wasn't borscht) had arrived minutes earlier, and like much of the cuisine on the trip, it wasn't showing up on the Food Network anytime soon. And I assure you, these men weren't "just into my meal."

Dan, Robert, and I are now thinking about our families back home, the vision of a shirtless Vladimir Putin riding horseback, and what Liam Neeson would do in this precarious situation.

But there's Jay Onrait, just loving every second of the scene like a pig in shit.

He's providing running commentary, cherishing it all. Jay's taking note of what kind of "darts" these guys are smoking (Sobranie, I'd later learn, was the brand). He's digging their 1980s *Family Ties*–era outfits (Note: Michael J. Fox . . . Canadian). He's fascinated by the way they're alternating drags of nicotine and bites of food. Jay Onrait does not want to leave the bar just yet. Maybe ever.

I swear, we'd still be at that table right now if he had it his way. He knew we'd be talking about those four Russian men and their cigarillos the rest of our lives, and he just wanted the moment to last forever.

He saw an amazingly humorous situation in what—I assure you—was not the slightest bit humorous at the time.

And that's Jay Onrait.

He is as charismatic, as magnetic, and as *fun* a guy as you could ever ask to be around. What you see on television (the rare nights he and Dan actually decide to work and are not off doing paid speaking engagements for 300 people in Manitoba) is what you get *off*-camera. If there's a sad clown side or darkness to him, I haven't seen it. The dude makes me laugh every day.

Jay's got this great bit where he puts on a fake sports announcer's voice. It's really early '90s, really affected, and really over the top. I love this voice and he knows it. I'll throw out a long-retired hockey player (German Titov!), an event (David Wells' perfect game!), a now-defunct team (the 2003 Atlanta Thrashers!), a fake MSNBC commentator (Craig Tomatoes)—anything—and he'll, on demand, break into this voice and give me the goods. It slays me every time.

Nice dude, too, this Jay Onrait. I had a birthday recently. I didn't tell anyone at Fox Sports about it. Sure enough, Jay and his wife, Chobi, sent me a $50 gift certificate to the Olive Garden. They know I like their breadsticks.

As for the whole book thing? As they say in Canada, "eh."

I read Jay's first attempt at a book, *Anchorboy*, over the course of the 2014 NFL season. In between talking about deflated footballs, following and covering Roger Goodell's toughest twelve months on the job, and travelling thousands and thousands of miles on airplanes, I got to know "the tall one" from his words and stories.

Fun read, yes, but I'll be honest—I don't really care about any of the shows he was ever on before he got to the United States ("The Big, Giant Lunch!"), I am not familiar with any of his former co-hosts (CFL legend Morris "the Wingnut" O'Shaughnessy!), and I cannot relate to his "son of a small-town Canadian pharmacist does good" story of triumph and Canadian cable TV dominance.

Jay's *first* memoir, I assumed, would be more than enough of a contribution to the literary world. His fans couldn't really *need* much more. Shit, I was impressed when I saw it was more than 1,300 words.

And yet, here we are, with volume two!

In a recent phone conversation, Jay casually referred to a bowel movement of his as "the colour of the Oakland Raiders' home jerseys." He pronounces the word *pasta* so wrong that it makes me cringe. He loves such off-the-radar, underproduced, horrible indie-hipster music that most times, I think he's just making the band names up to screw with me. His love of the 1990s post-Gretzky Edmonton Oilers is, at times, borderline alarming (hello, "Sweet" Billy Ranford).

And yet, he makes me laugh like few other people in the world.

I'm honoured to be writing this foreword and truly honoured (#blessed) every day I get to work alongside the guy on Fox Sports 1.

Oh, and guess what? Dan lost all that weight he put on in Russia. Robert did, too. And we made it out of that dimly lit restaurant just fine. No harm done. No problems whatsoever.

And Jay was right. There are countless days when I wish we were all still at that table, just soaking in that experience all over again.

Now, go ahead, light up a Sobranie cigarette, take your pants off, and enjoy this book. If you didn't get enough stories in Jay's first book about being a famous TV personality and the many times he was nearly fired, there's plenty more for you here.

Cue the music, Patrick.

DANCE.

Chapter 1

The Origins of My Depravity

I started masturbating at the age of eight. *Eight!* I didn't really know what I was doing, but every single night, purely on instinct, I would yank down the bottoms of my pajamas, and using the index finger and thumb of *both hands*, I'd yank my tiny pecker up and down until I felt the sensation of a tiny orgasm. No fluid would be secreted, of course, but it became my nightly routine. I started so young I can only assume I was masturbating to album covers from my mother's record collection or perhaps the curvy and muscular green specimen that was She-Hulk.

My father owned a drugstore in town, and until he sold it, the concept of paying for comics and magazines was completely foreign to me. I remember the first time I went to get a magazine after he had sold the store. Four dollars and ninety-nine cents for *Sports Illustrated*? Are they *nuts*? It also took some time to adjust to reading magazines with covers on them. Every week in the store we would take all the unsold magazines, rip off the covers, and send the covers back to the distributor for credit. The cover-torn magazines were now free for all the employees to take for themselves. This included the two adult magazines my father allowed to be sold in the store: *Playboy* and *Penthouse*.

Playboy was always pretty tame. Even now I like to read it on planes. I get a kick out of it. I try to be a bit covert and keep the cover hidden from view, but inevitably as I'm flipping pages, reading the surprisingly great articles and interviews, I'll come across a photo spread involving two naked co-eds in football gear and I will look across the aisle to see a sixty-two-year-old woman looking at me like, "Does this look like your private den of sin? Shame on you!"

Penthouse was a different story. It had actual photo spreads of men and women engaged in sexual acts—*with* penetration. Not to mention the infamous *Penthouse* "Letters" that filled the first few pages of the magazine. "Actual letters from actual readers," which was complete bullshit, but a real erotic read for a twelve-year-old kid just discovering sexuality. From time to time, I managed to sneak a few *Penthouse* magazines away from my dad's store to the privacy of my bedroom, where I would become engrossed in tale after tale of housewives whose husbands had allowed them to be defrocked by their next door neighbour. Erotic literature of its day, I suppose.

Through these experiences, I became enamoured with pornography, but unlike today when a kid can just learn their parents' password for the "bad" websites and cable channels, there was really no way for me to watch pornographic films. That is, unless I got the assistance of good friends with satellite dishes.

Here's how it worked: I would bring in a blank VHS tape to

school and ask one of my friends to take it home and set his VCR to record at night while his parents were asleep. In the morning he would pop the tape out of the machine, put it in his backpack, and bring it to me at school. Using a clever system of deception that will now be copied by porno-pirates across the globe, I would carefully collect the extra VHS tape labels and keep them in my bedroom. Then, upon receiving the sweet treasure that was a new VHS tape with FP on it (Fresh Porn), I would label the tape with something like "WWF Saturday Night's Main Event," which was the popular NBC wrestling show of the day that would often replace Saturday Night Live in the late-night lineup when Hulk Hogan et al. were at their peak of popularity. There was simply no chance my parents or sister would pop this tape into the VCR to check out the latest embarrassing loss by wrestler Koko B. Ware, the one who brought a live parrot into the ring. Therefore, I would often leave these tapes stacked up right next to our other VHS tapes underneath the TV, alongside such classic films of the day as *Night Shift* and *Smokey and the Bandit*, so they were in a convenient spot whenever I found myself alone in the house. It may seem like a lot of effort now, but it never really felt like work—it felt like a necessary part of life.

The funny thing is it took me a long time to find true joy out of masturbation. I realize that's a pretty good "pull quote" for this book—no pun intended—but I'm serious. The whole premise of the Catholic doctrine is that you are a horrible, miserable sinner who is unworthy of God's love, and each and every week God decides to forgive you for your horrible, miserable sins and allow you to enter his "house" and worship him. Catholic guilt has been examined and dissected by therapists for years, but it basically boils down to this: Catholics feel guilty about enjoying *anything* because every

Sunday they are told that they are sinning too much and unworthy of their creator's love.

Now, let's back up, as I discover the harmless and medically healthy practice of masturbation in my preteen years. I was so riddled with Catholic guilt and, worse, genuinely convinced that God was watching me, like *really* watching me, that I couldn't even really enjoy myself like a normal teenager. When I was actually wanking off, that was about as great as life got at the time. But when I was finished, the guilt was so overwhelming I'd almost be in tears. I would look up, to heaven presumably, and beg the Lord's forgiveness for what I had just done. Not only that, but I would talk to him as if I were a crack addict who had hit the pipe one last time and was about to go cold turkey. "Lord, I am so sorry, and if you forgive me this *one last time*, I promise, *promise*, that I will never ever masturbate again." The next day I'd say the exact same thing, probably in the exact same spot—the guest bathroom, which was far enough away from the rest of the house that I could be assured the most privacy. It was a small powder room, appropriately not much bigger than a confessional booth. One evening, my father burst in and there I was, pants down around my ankles, face red as an apple, yanking away like I was trying to start a tiny lawnmower between my legs. He took one look at me, turned around, and walked out.

Back in the '80s, almost every hotel room in North America was equipped with a Spectravision cable box on top of the set that allowed guests to watch pay-per-view movies—which included *adult* movies. Schoolyard legend of the day had it that you wouldn't get charged for any movies as long as you watched less than five minutes and then quickly changed the channel. So one family vacation I decided to test the theory.

One summer when I was about thirteen, my parents, sister, and I piled into the Chevy Suburban and headed out toward Penticton in the interior of British Columbia. We made it all the way to Banff on our first day and decided to stay the night at a nice hotel in town. After dinner, my parents and sister went to bed and I was allowed to stay up to watch TV. We weren't in a suite or anything. We were all in the same room, one double bed and two singles in less than 300 square feet. And one television.

I sat at the edge of my bed, with my entire family dozing off behind me. Satisfied that everyone else was locked in a deep sleep, I began to test the theory that had been presented to me. I flipped back and forth to an adult film starring Tom Byron, Joey Silvera, and an actress named Raven, about a rock star and his manager and the girl who got between them—literally. I would watch for less than five minutes, always keeping one eye on the clock, then turn back to TSN or MuchMusic. I continued to look back at my family who, had they opened their eyes at any point, would have been staring *directly at the television.*

At some point I crashed, probably after masturbating in the bathroom, and slumbered with a smile, confidently knowing I had successfully defeated the system and watched a lot of great adult entertainment—for free! Life was good. That is, until the next morning when we got ready for the second day of driving to the Okanagan. We packed everything into the Suburban and Dad returned to the front desk to check out. After five minutes we started to wonder where he was. After ten minutes my mom was starting to get concerned. After fifteen minutes I was shitting my pants. I knew exactly what was holding him up.

Twenty minutes later, Dad wandered back out to the Suburban with a scowl on his face. He got in the car and let out a long sigh.

"What happened? What took you so long?" asked my mom.

Dad turned around to face me.

"Did you order up a movie or two last night after we all went to bed, Jay?" He had that familiar, frightening tone of a man who was doing everything he could to keep from exploding with rage.

"Nope, I didn't order anything," I lied.

"The lady at the front desk said our room ordered three adult movies last night. You have no idea about that, huh?"

I looked around the car. My mom had a look of profound disappointment. My father had a look of barely suppressed anger. My sister had a look that said: You ordered porn in our room while we were all sleeping? *What the fuck is wrong with you?*

I had to fess up. "Yeah, it was me."

Then I completely spilled the beans. I explained that someone in my class had told me I could watch these movies for free if I only watched for five minutes, but obviously I had watched for longer than five minutes at least three times and, wow, was I ever sorry. I would rather have been knee deep in a field full of cow shit than in that car at that moment. I was paralyzed with embarrassment.

"Next time," said Dad, "just tell us if you want to watch something."

Oh, sure. I can just imagine how that conversation would have gone:

"Hey, Dad, I've turned into an obsessively horny thirteen-year-old with no ability to control my sexual urges. I may also already be addicted to pornography. You wouldn't mind springing for a couple adult films at the hotel that I will watch on the edge of the bed while you all slumber close by, would you? Great!"

At the time I went to university, the Internet was still not widely available. So, having long before accepted that I was a sinner and a masturbation addict, I was excited to discover I could walk into the Rogers Video on 82nd Avenue in Edmonton and rent adult films to enjoy in the comfort of my own home. This was a wonderful time for the adult film industry as Jenna Jameson was about to explode onto the scene—again, no pun intended. There was a wealth of great material to choose from, produced by classic studios like Vivid and Wicked. The only problem was that I felt even more ashamed renting the videos than I ever did when actually masturbating. That's because the setup at Rogers Video was designed to make you feel the maximum amount of embarrassment possible.

The Rogers on 82nd Avenue was a massive video store, very standard at the time, still renting VHS tapes in 1992. After I made it past all the copies of *The Goonies* and *Dances with Wolves*, I would walk all the way to the back of the store where there was a *tiny* room with a curtain. I would part the curtain and there, arranged on shelves like little filthy treasures, were the adult films. There would always be one or two other guys in the room already examining the available titles, and they would briefly look up to acknowledge me and then turn their eyes back to the tapes as if to say, "You're no better than me. We're all in this shame spiral together."

After I selected my tape, or more likely *tapes*, I would make sure to circle back through the main area of the store and pick up one or two "regular" movies to supplement my filth. I would take care to use those normal movies to sandwich the adult movies so the clerk might not be totally frightened when I put them down on the counter.

Then I would take my place in what always seemed to be a long lineup and survey the other patrons around me. I was always hoping, praying, that the lady right behind me had some sort of hearing disorder. This was because it seemed to be Rogers Video employee policy to say the name of every single movie that passed through their hands as loudly as possible. This would result in a profoundly embarrassing moment when I went to pay that sounded a little something like this:

CLERK: *Indiana Jones and the Temple of Doom*! What a classic! You've seen it, right?

JAY: Oh, yeah. Love it.

CLERK: Just amazing. So violent. What else do we have here? *Robocop*. Awesome!

JAY: So underrated.

CLERK: Totally. What else? *The Scarlett Mistress*? Okay . . .

JAY: I'm in a bit of a rush . . .

CLERK: One more. *Busty Backdoor Nurses*? Uh, will that be all?

JAY (ashamed): Yes.

CLERK: Oh, I missed one. *Big Cheek Freaks*. Wow.

JAY: Can we hurry this up?

CLERK: So we have *Temple of Doom*, *Robocop*, *Scarlett Mistress*, *Busty Backdoor Nurses*, and *Big Cheek Freaks* . . .

JAY: Like I said, I'm in a bit of a rush.

By that point, everyone in line was giving me the same look—a look that said, "So, you're not really going to be watching *Robocop* or *Indiana Jones* are you? You horrible pervert. You filth-ridden spank jockey. Take your disgusting tapes and get out of this store."

Then I would pack up the tapes and keep my head down as I scurried off to my car, feeling a combination of debilitating shame and joyous elation—and mostly just thankful there weren't any children in the lineup.

Chapter 2

The New Kid in Town

Before I moved to Athabasca at the age of ten I had never been in a fight in my life. In my first year in that town, I was in at least four. It probably didn't help that I wasn't exactly trying to be inconspicuous.

The previous summer my next door neighbour Daryl told me his cousin Colin thought we should both be wearing skinny leather ties. Colin was considered very cool because he was in high school. "Colin told me pink is the cool colour now," said Daryl. Colin had just returned from Edmonton—"the City"—where he had been buying back-to-school clothes, and basically anything he said to us about how to dress was gospel. "Pink leather ties, that's what everyone is wearing."

So as the new school year approached, my parents took me to West Edmonton Mall for my own back-to-school shopping and I insisted on going to Zazoo, a store that would become well known two or three years later as a go-to spot for the latest Zubaz sweatpants. At Zazoo I stocked up on ties. Not just in pink but also in black, blue, and red—all skinny, all leather. It might sound very hipster now, but it was a little weird for a ten-year-old. I think the popularity of Alex P. Keaton, Michael J. Fox's conservative character on *Family Ties*, led me to believe that wearing ties to school in grade five would be a wise decision. Instead, it put a giant target on my back.

A few weeks into fifth grade, I participated in an ill-advised arm wrestling contest one day after school. My long, lanky arms provided extra leverage, and miraculously I placed second. I was beaming with pride as my new friend Troy Dubie described me as "pretty tough," especially since Troy was a real cowboy, a future bull rider. It seemed like everything was going my way until one day, when walking to my dad's new drugstore after school, I was suddenly cornered by Rory Langevin, easily the biggest kid in my class. I had heard of him but never met him, and now he was introducing himself to me the only way he knew how.

"Hey, are you Jay?" he asked.

"Y-y-yeah?" I replied, reluctantly.

"Some guys were saying you were tougher than me today, so we're gonna fight after school tomorrow. Right outside the gym. Then we'll see who's tougher."

"What?" I literally almost shit my pants right then and there. A wave of panic swept through my body and my stomach tightened. Why had I entered the world's stupidest fifth-grade arm wrestling contest?

"Do you want to go bike riding sometime?" asked Rory, a quick changer of subjects.

"Uh, no. I have to get back," I replied absent-mindedly. Get back to where? I had no idea. I had to get away from this monolith that had me pinned against the wall by the post office.

"Okay. Remember tomorrow. *Boom!*" And with that, he walked away.

Good God. I had unwillingly been placed in a main event title fight with a *major* weight class discrepancy. Every other fight I'd been in had been against someone fairly close to my body size, but now I was about to take on the Goliath of the Northern Prairies, and the whole school was going to see me get destroyed. Tears began to stream down my cheeks as I stumbled—*stumbled*—down the remaining stretch of alley toward the back of my dad's store. As I waited for him to finish work so I could get a ride home, I wandered around the store in a daze, flipping through comics, every inch of my body filled with unbridled terror.

I was practically inconsolable on the drive home as I explained the situation to my dad. Once we were in the house, my parents tried to calm me down.

"Why would someone say that to you? What did you do to him? Just come straight home from school." *Moms!* If only life were as easy for their children as they wanted it to be in their heads. After she walked away to finish making dinner, my dad quietly offered me words of advice for dealing with a playground combat situation.

"Remember: Quick jabs to the face." Got it. *Quick jabs to the face.* I would be sure to remember that as Rory took one big swing at my chest and sent me flying back ten feet as my fellow fifth-grade students laughed uproariously.

I didn't sleep much that night. The next day, I awoke with a feeling of dread the likes of which I had never experienced before. *Dead man walking.* My father dropped me off at school and wished me luck, probably wondering what my face would look like at the end of the day. I went through the motions in my morning class like a young zombie who had just been bitten and was getting used to a catatonic state. Gym class was right before noon, and Rory was going to be out there playing dodgeball either alongside or against me. Maybe I could fake a dodgeball injury and he would see it and spare me a beating.

I wandered into the tiny gym and went to sit on the stage while the rest of my fellow students gathered. None of us were changing into gym clothes yet. We were too young for that. We were too young to really sweat anyway. We'd just run around like idiots and then return to class in the same clothes. That was the routine. Suddenly, out of the corner of my eye I saw Rory, a hulking presence in hand-me-down jeans, running shoes, and an oversized T-shirt. He was headed right for me. My eyes bugged out in terror as he sat down beside me on the stage. He couldn't have had a more pleasant disposition. *What the fuck is wrong with this asshole?* I thought. Why was he so calm and measured about ruining my day and my reputation and my face in this new town and this new school where I was doing so well? He opened his mouth and spoke slowly:

"Hey, I heard we're going to be on the same hockey team," he stated proudly, like he was actually happy about this.

"Uh, we are?" I wasn't really capable of forming coherent sentences with this bully sitting beside me, talking to me like I was his friend when just hours later he was going to use his big bear paws to dent my delicate face.

"Yeah, my mom said you're on my team."

His *mom*? How did *that* subject come up? Did Rory get home after interrogating me in the alley by the post office and tell his parents about the skinny new kid in town he was going to massacre the next day? Only to have his mom inform him that the skinny new kid was going to be playing defence on the second power play? This whole conversation was highly bizarre. Then Rory turned his head to one side, tilted it even, like he was actually thinking, as if there were actually thoughts going on in his oversized noggin.

"Hey, do you really want to have that fight after school?" he asked.

"N-no," I mumbled. I was a broken young fella, so happy and relieved, but too rattled to enjoy being let off the hook.

"Me neither, see you at hockey!" And with that he leapt off the stage and into the fray of dodgeballs and squeaking sneakers.

Of all the times I had been rocked by violent diarrhea while away from the cozy confines of my toilet—and by now you have probably guessed that situation occurs frequently—nothing compared to the relief I felt that day when Rory called off the fight that afternoon. I no longer had to worry about Rory, other than the fact that he couldn't skate and was a real detriment to the success of our hockey team.

Chapter 3

Dopebusters: The Case of the Leather Jacket Gang

The email chain was pretty innocuous. The subject line read: "President at Cameron Indoor Stadium." The first email was from Dustyn Waite, one of our researchers on *Fox Sports Live*, and it was inspired by President Obama's upcoming visit to Duke University to watch their men's basketball team play.

"The only previous U.S. president to appear at Cameron Indoor Stadium was Ronald Reagan in 1988."

To which Ian Martin, one of our production assistants, replied: "Next sentence: 'Reagan, the nation's 40th president, spoke during an anti-drug seminar.'"

This was followed by a reply from Andy Meyer, another of our researchers a little older than the rest of the staff. Okay, a lot older.

Like my age. We had all dubbed him "Handsome Andy" for his matinee idol good looks and jovial nature. Andy wrote: "Just say no, Ian. Just say no . . ."

And the email chain stopped abruptly there.

He got nothing.

No further replies, no LOLs. I hadn't been responding to the chain so I assumed the conversation had simply just died out, but later that evening when I ran into Handsome Andy in the hallway near my offacle (not quite an office, not quite a cubicle—the walls didn't go up to the ceiling, but there were walls and it was better than fighting for a computer with the interns like I did back at TSN), I mentioned to Andy how much I enjoyed his "Just say no" comment.

"You're the only one! No one else even gave it a mention."

"Really? No one else understood it?" I said, perplexed.

"No one said a thing. No one replied. I feel really old! I made a really old reference and no one got it. You and I were the only ones."

I understood exactly what he meant. Thirty years ago making a "Just Say No" reference would have been met with a laugh, or acknowledgement at the very least. Now, it was just as much a promotional campaign memory as "Where's the Beef" or "Calgon Take Me Away" (even I was too young for that last one).

If the 1970s were cocaine's big coming out party, then the 1980s were the depressing morning-after crash and comedown. So many musicians, actors, Hollywood executives, and general douchebags who'd experimented with the drug after the '60s were over and thought that it could do no more harm than smoking a joint suddenly found themselves addicted and strung out and in need of serious help.

One of the most infamous stories comes from the ultimate cocaine-obsessive band of the late '70s, the Stevie Nicks/Lindsey

Buckingham lineup of Fleetwood Mac, who were apparently given rations of the devil's dandruff before they went on stage: one Heineken bottlecapful each. That led to the best story about Nicks in which her cocaine addiction became so bad she burned a hole in her nasal passageway (true), leading to her demanding that her assistant administer the drug suppository-style into her behind with a straw (denied by her, of course).

If you were like me, a child born in the 1970s who really came of age in the 1980s, you were subjected to an incredibly effective advertising campaign meant to make you think that drugs were *no longer cool.*

In his book and subsequent documentary *The Kid Stays in the Picture*, former Paramount Pictures chief Robert Evans discusses his descent into cocaine addiction and subsequent arrest that led to, as part of his sentence, an all-star version of an anti-drug video featuring some of the biggest movie and television stars of the day singing a "We Are the World"–style anti-drug song. The video also featured a confused looking Bob Hope. I can only imagine how strange it must have been to be a part of that shoot, explaining to an aged Hope why the anti-drug message was so important. Such videos were pretty much commonplace at the time. Big-name Hollywood players like Evans, who had their wrists slapped, suddenly became contrite anti-drug crusaders. Then there were the child stars of the day like Soleil Moon Frye (Punky Brewster) and Ricky Schroder (Rick Stratton from *Silver Spoons*). They were part of the generation that was recruited for the "Just Say No" campaign, which was championed by then first lady Nancy Reagan.

Seeing these child stars, all my age, so vehemently anti-drug really worked. It had a profound effect on me and my peers. In our minds cocaine was truly evil, and trying it once was a one-way ticket to the gutter. But it didn't stop there. Even pot, in my tender elementary school mind, was an addictive and evil substance that would surely lead me to ruin. Once again it was the prevalence of anti-marijuana commercials that drew me to this conclusion. Teenagers shown throwing away lives full of massive potential because they couldn't resist taking another toke. All those campaigns were terrifying and, it should be said, extremely effective.

By the time I reached fifth grade, I had never so much as seen a recreational drug of any kind in my life and I didn't want to. That's how deeply the "Just Say No" campaign had affected me. The aftermath of unbridled excess from the late 1970s had turned everyone into preaching teetotalers in the 1980s—at least the ones who were on NBC's prime-time lineup. It was simply *not cool* to do drugs in our little ten-year-old minds, and it was up to us to keep our school, the only elementary school in town, drug free and safe from the influence of leather-clad hooligans who might try to push their illegal demon weed on fellow students with weaker, less informed minds on the subject.

When I was in grade five, we had a group of grade seven students crammed into our school while they waited for classrooms at the high school to be renovated.

Since we had an extra 120 students squeezed into our tiny school, and since those extra 120 students were now too old to be hanging around on the playground or playing soccer in the nearby field, many of them simply loafed around like a bunch of ne'er-do-wells. Between discussions about the hot new television show of the moment, *Miami Vice*, one group caught our attention: a bunch of dudes sporting leather jackets and dirty jeans who walked around like they were semi-comatose. Each and every noon hour they would make their way into the forest that surrounded our school. That's right; I said "forest that surrounded our school." The school was situated right on the edge of town, so there was plenty of opportunity to wander into the trees and get into trouble.

One day just after we moved to town, my sister and our new neighbour Karina Gregory wandered into the forest after school and discovered a nearby creek that flowed from the mighty Athabasca River. The creek was absolutely spectacular: fresh, clean water that was so delicious looking we all scooped it up and took a drink. "Why not just live here forever?" we wondered as we planned our new utopian society where we would forage fresh berries for food and wipe our bums with the leaves of the poplar trees that grew so plentifully around us. It all seemed so idyllic. We could leave behind school, we could leave behind leather ties, and we could all start again right there in the forest next to town—possibly in the nude.

Eventually the sun went down and we decided to head back, getting a little lost along the way before finally making it home. Once we bid goodbye to Karina, my sister and I walked up the steps to the front door of our little rented duplex. My parents had wanted to buy a home, but the newly opened Athabasca University—a correspondence school—meant that every available property had already been snatched up. We opened the front door and my mom's eyes were like saucers.

"Where have you two been?" she asked frantically.

Before we could manage an answer, my dad emerged from the back bedroom area with a fire and rage in his eyes the likes of which I had never seen.

"Where the hell were you two?" His voice was not quite a yell, just a notch below; it was the best he could manage in that situation. "We have been calling around, worried sick! Did you not think we would wonder where you were?"

In this day and age before cellphones allowed parents to keep watch on their children like Big Brother, in a town where we were able to roam freely and play anywhere and everywhere we liked, we had finally pushed the boundaries too far. Apparently, my parents had come to the conclusion that their children had been kidnapped and would never be seen again. They had just moved to a new town with their family, and I can only imagine the thoughts that were running through my mother's mind as she frantically called my dad to come home from the drugstore and help her look for the ten-year-old and the eight-year-old who had somehow gone missing and were a full hour late for dinner on a weeknight. We were grounded for the first time in our lives.

The forest was not our friend that day.

But that didn't mean we stayed away. Instead, for the rest of the summer we went back into the forest every chance we got. It became our home away from home, our own private, secret hideout. We just made sure we kept an eye on our Swatches so we would be home in time for dinner.

So when we began observing these leather-jacket-sporting hooligans disappearing into the trees every day, we decided it was up to us to defend the forest from whatever shady deeds they were committing. We were convinced that the Leather Jacket Gang (as we began calling them) was heading into the trees to . . . wait for it:

Smoke marijuana.

It was time to get to work. Inspired by the "Just Say No" campaign, we decided to call ourselves the Dopebusters. Finally, we had a purpose for our recess and noon-hour breaks.

My friend Robin Bobocel was an only child—a rarity in a small prairie town where families usually had at least two children since so many people lived on farms and acreages, and boredom was sure to cause an isolated child to drive their parents absolutely crazy.

Robin was different. Robin was an accident. I know this because he would remind us about it all the time. His parents had obviously told him at a ridiculously young age, but Robin had such an easygoing disposition that nothing ever seemed to bother him— not even his parents informing him that his entire presence on our planet was simply the result of too much red wine and too little caution with birth control. Robin was as relaxed and happy a kid as I ever met. He had clearly never wanted for anything. A visit to his "playroom" next to his bedroom at his family's house just a few kilometres outside of town was like a visit to the nearest Toys "R" Us.

Robin had the latest of everything and was also one of the first kids I knew with satellite television. He used to come to school and regale us with exciting tales of MTV beamed in from the United States, while we were stuck with plain old MuchMusic in Canada. Years later he would be one of the only students to actually receive a new car for his sixteenth birthday, a forest green Jeep YJ that made our jaws drop as he casually pulled up to school one day cranking the beats of Sir Mix-a-Lot.

Back in fifth grade, though, Robin was a valuable member of the Dopebusters team, because in addition to the toys and the satellite dish and the trampoline in his expansive backyard, Robin was also the only one of us who had his own camera.

After several recess breaks spent performing covert surveillance on the Leather Jacket Gang, we decided we needed actual photographic evidence to bring these "perps" to justice. No way were we going to stand by and simply spy on these rule-breaking drug fiends; we needed to teach them and their kind a lesson—that drugs of any kind would not be tolerated in our school.

During one particularly fruitful spying session, we hung around long enough to watch the Leather Jacket Gang leave early before the bell rang, giving us the opportunity to check for evidence left behind in the little forest clearing where they sat around, laughing at their own jokes—a little too hard for our liking. Once the jacket squad had cleared out, we carefully snuck down to the clearing, and it was there that my fellow Dopebuster, Kevin Meyer, found . . . wait for it . . . an empty container of cough syrup! The boys were drinking sizzurp years before it was cool with hip hop stars and Justin Bieber. Taking out one of the Glad sandwich bags I had stuffed in my jacket pocket that morning while my mom was preparing my lunch, I carefully scooped up the empty cough syrup container to be stored back in my cubbyhole for safe keeping, not taking into account that if our teachers or principals actually considered drinking cough syrup some sort of crime, then I was basically putting the evidence in my own possession. It was like someone finding a murder weapon and putting their fingerprints all over it. Columbo I was not. I was not even Angela Lansbury from *Murder She Wrote*.

But even with the cough syrup bottle, we still felt we needed photographic evidence. So the next day, Robin, Kevin, and I, plus the other idiots we'd convinced to join us in this ridiculous venture, all snuck into the trees near the school at lunch hour and resumed our stakeout. The goal was simple: Get a picture of these ne'er-do-wells smoking, drinking, or ingesting actual drugs so we could take it to our teacher, Mr. Galonka, and rid our once clean and serene school of the scourge of drugs forever. We watched the clock impatiently, thirsting for justice, knowing that nothing was going to stand in our way of putting these scumbags behind bars.

When that bell finally rang we tore up the hill as fast as our ten-year-old legs could carry us, hoping to beat the Leather Jacket Gang to their favourite spot. We set up shop near the clearing—dangerously close—and waited.

Sure enough, a few minutes later the Leather Jacket Gang showed up and sat on tree stumps in a circle like they were about to start a campfire. One of them fired up a lighter, and a billow of smoke wafted through the air.

The demon weed!

This was our moment. Illegal drug activity was taking place right before our very eyes and now was our chance to stomp it out.

Sadly, this was years before camera phones could have captured the action with the silence required for such a covert operation. Robin's camera was not so quiet. Robin was on his elbows, clicking away, and lying on my stomach just a few feet away I thought it all sounded dangerously loud. How could the Leather Jacket Gang not hear Robin snapping away with his camera like a young Annie Leibovitz?

The Gang continued to smoke away while Robin snapped his pictures. When he was comfortably satisfied that he had captured enough photographic evidence to put these guys behind bars where they deserved to be, Robin signalled for us all to sneak away in the opposite direction so we could make our escape. Then after school we would quickly get these pictures developed at my dad's drugstore and bring the photographic evidence to the appropriate authorities, probably the Royal Canadian Mounted Police.

Just as I put my hand down to slowly and quietly prop myself up and leave, I heard a voice—the most terrifying voice I had ever heard. Menacing, ominous, it came from one of the Leather Jacket Gang, the one with his back to us. He didn't even turn around when he said:

"You guys are gonna get it."

We had been caught, and now there was nothing to do but panic.

We all sprang up in unison and ran, screaming at the top of our lungs the entire time.

All the way down the hill we ran, pushing aside tree branches, stepping on leaves and dog shit, practically falling all over each other in our attempt to flee the scene. It wasn't exactly every man for himself, but if you were to have witnessed us emerging from the trees that day you would have assumed we had all been held against our will in those bushes for weeks and had just now found our escape. That was the level of unbridled terror in our eyes. Our fellow students looked at us like we were completely and totally insane.

We sprinted to the doorway of the school and ran inside toward our home classroom, where Mr. Galonka would surely appreciate our tale and keep us safe from the pursuers who were about to be exposed to the entire world for their drug use and general bad influence.

But there was no one behind us.

No one.

They hadn't even bothered to chase after us. They just didn't care. They were happy to put the fear of God into us and that was that. They went on drinking their sizzurp and smoking what was likely one of their father's cigarettes. It probably wasn't even dope.

We had never really gotten a good look at their faces, so we had no idea who they even were. There weren't many kids wearing leather ties at that school, but there were plenty of twelve- and thirteen-year-olds wearing bad leather jackets. We never did find out who the real Leather Jacket Gang was.

After that embarrassing conclusion to the investigation, we wisely closed up our detective agency and the Dopebusters became nothing but a memory from those few weeks in grade five when we suddenly became the least cool school kids in North America.

Chapter 4

The Sweat and the Fury

Growing up, my father didn't make me do many chores around the house, but my one regular responsibility was mowing our one-acre back lawn about once a week during the summer months in Alberta. (For those not from Alberta, the "summer months" are May to August, and maybe September if you're lucky. Truthfully, they may just be June to August. Okay, *just* August.) I actually enjoyed mowing the lawn because I would throw on the foam-covered headphones, slap a tape into the Walkman, and groove out to some of the hottest hip hop sounds of the day. This being the late '80s and early '90s, that would include such seminal releases as Big Daddy Kane's *It's a Big Daddy Thing*; Digital Underground's *Humpty Dance*; Public Enemy's *It Takes a Nation of Millions to Hold Us Back* and *Fear of a Black Planet*; A Tribe Called Quest's *The Low End Theory*; N.W.A's *Straight Outta Compton* and *Efil4zaggin*; and Beastie Boys rivals 3rd Bass's *The Cactus Album*. I was into hip hop at an early enough age to have regularly listened to MC Hammer *before* "You Can't Touch This" (the *Let's Get It Started* album) and Sir Mix-a-Lot *before* "Baby Got Back" (the *Swass* album).

When it comes to hip hop's all-time greatest MCs, I'm often disheartened to see Big Daddy Kane fail to get mentioned with regularity. Maybe it's because he simply faded out of the spotlight. I was somewhat disappointed in Kane's *It's a Big Daddy Thing* follow-up, *Taste of Chocolate*, but there was one hilarious song on the new album called "Big Daddy vs. Dolemite" where Kane traded increasingly profane barbs with the '70s era Blaxploitation comedian. The song was so foul that it shocked even me—and I was listening regularly to Andrew Dice Clay at the time. I once made the mistake of forgetting to eject the tape out of the deck in my father's 1990 Chevy Silverado, which we used to deliver prescriptions to the local nursing homes in town. When he drove home that night he got into the truck, turned the key, and at full volume heard Dolemite say something about wanting to take out his shiny dick and tear up some lady's old grey ass. I can just imagine how shocked and borderline frightened he was after a day of counting pills and dispensing advice about enemas. My father never really paid attention to the music I was listening to. He didn't seem to listen to music at all except for perhaps the soundtrack to *Joseph and the Amazing Technicolor Dreamcoat*. So I was seriously taken aback when Dad stormed into the house that evening shouting, "What the heck is that music you were listening to in the truck? Pretty foul!" He was not amused. I didn't even know what he was referring to until the word "Dolemite" was uttered. The situation could have been a lot worse—I mean, I could have left a 2 Live Crew album in the truck.

2 Live Crew was a four-person group started by Miami impresario Luther Campbell that made waves with their pornographic rhymes

as opposed to the gangster rap world created and cultivated by the likes of N.W.A. Their entire debut album, *As Nasty as They Wanna Be*, was like an audiobook for an African-American pornographic film set to programmed drum beats. Their huge debut single, "Me So Horny," was an exercise in nuance and subtlety. Naturally, I was a big fan. So much so that when my friends and I got word that 2 Live Crew was opening for Tone Loc at the Dinwoodie Bar at the University of Alberta, I begged my father to drive us all in to see it. Amazingly, he agreed.

The Dinwoodie was not a regular concert venue for the likes of my friends. We had pretty much been shackled to Northlands Coliseum where the Edmonton Oilers played. That's where Edmonton hosted stars of the day like Poison, Bon Jovi, Skid Row, and yes, Janet Jackson, who busted out some serious moves in a Martin Gelinas Edmonton Oilers jersey on her *Control* tour.

The Dinwoodie was an altogether different venue. It was for all intents and purposes a bar with a performance stage that often hosted improv comedy shows. The bar did host a few concerts from up-and-coming indie rock bands and Canadian acts, but it was a somewhat strange choice for the performers of such blockbuster hits as "Wild Thing" and "Funky Cold Medina."

The pairing of Tone Loc and 2 Live Crew was very strange in and of itself. 2 Live Crew was the biggest purveyor of filth in the day, the target of Tipper Gore's censorship campaign, "Parental Advisory" stickers plastered all over their tapes and CDs. Tone Loc was about as vanilla as they came. No one was fooled by his "Wild Thing" video and the subject matter of the hit song. This was a fat, lovable, mostly agreeable fellow who wasn't out to offend anybody. In other words, he was absolutely *not* cool. He was a Top 40 rapper—even this hip hop loving prairie boy knew that. I didn't own his album, and I had no real desire to see him in concert. But as soon as I heard that 2 Live Crew was opening for him, the tickets were purchased over the phone and plans were made to drive into "the City" to see these crazy Floridians for ourselves.

We were actually not that used to general admission concerts. The venue was one big room with a stage at the side. All my friends were fairly tall, and we quickly realized what an advantage height would be for us at general admission concerts in the future and how much of a disadvantage that would be for those who stood behind us. We shimmied and squirmed our way through the mass of white, pimple-faced Edmonton hip hop fans toward the stage until we were standing directly in front, blissfully unaware that our eardrums were about to get their first real test of limitless programmed drum beats and profane hip hop shouting. We were young and full of stamina, and we knew the words to every ridiculously foul number on the group's hit album, *As Nasty as They Wanna Be.*

Then we waited . . .

And waited . . .

And waited . . .

At first, we kind of appreciated that they were a little bit late; it gave the crowd an excuse to come together in encouragement—everyone started cheering and chanting, "2 Live Crew! 2 Live Crew!" But by the time a full hour went by, the crowd was starting to get restless, and by the time the second hour went past, that restless crowd was genuinely starting to get pissed off.

But even more than anger, that crowd was dying of thirst.

I had never been part of a group that was packed that tightly into a venue before. I hadn't paid attention as I was blissfully making my way to the front of the crowd, but as minute after minute went by with no sign of the group anywhere, I started to take notice of my surroundings. I was packed in way too tightly next to my friends, and everyone was starting to sweat. No air conditioning, lights blaring on the stage as two massive African-American security guards stood next to each other, arms folded, staring at the crowd. I wasn't craving anything to drink when I arrived at the Dinwoodie, but after that second hour went by every bit of hydration had finally left my pores and I desperately needed something—*anything*—to quench my thirst.

As two hours became two and a half, we began to wonder if the group was going to make it out onto the stage *at all*. At that point I would have literally traded my friends next to me for a sip of water—warm, dirty, it wouldn't have mattered. My lips and throat were so dry I stopped trying to make small talk with anyone around me. I stood helpless as the larger of the two security guards walked out from behind the curtain carrying a big bottle of aqua, which he proceeded to drink like he was an extra in the movie *Flashdance*, pouring the water over his head, as we watched, desperately wishing he would take pity and spray the crowd with his own cold spit. Five minutes later he came out with two more bottles of water, which we thought was some kind of ridiculous practical joke, and then proceeded to spray the crowd as we cheered in relief.

Word began to circulate through the crowd that the plane carrying 2 Live Crew, Tone Loc, and their respective posses had taken off late but had since arrived. Those of us new to the concert scene imagined all of them sprinting off their private jet on the tarmac of the Edmonton International Airport into a waiting stretch limousine.

"Step on it! We've been keeping hundreds of Northern Alberta hip hop fans waiting!" Tone Loc would shout to the driver, who would weave in and out of traffic at high speeds like a real-life game of *Spy Hunter*. Alas, like so many of my concert dreams that night, the concept of the artists rushing to a venue when they were late was also a pipe dream that was about to be shattered.

Moments later the water-soaked security guard once again came to the front of the stage to initial cheers that soon turned into jeers when he announced that "2 Live Crew are now eating their dinner and will be taking the stage shortly." Eating their dinner? Couldn't they have grabbed a few tacos from Taco Time on the way in? Patience was wearing thin. No one was under the illusion that Edmonton was a spot on the map where hip hop artists were going to perform with regularity, but still, those would-be gangsters were really trying our patience.

A half hour later, three full hours after they were scheduled to take the stage, DJ Mr. Mixx, one of the founders of the group, walked out to the turntables, and the crowd let out a relieved and desperate cheer. Finally, 2 Live Crew was about to hit the stage! But first we were treated to a special added bonus, presumably because we had waited for such a long time with such patience. Two neon-green-and-orange-bikini-clad African-American statuesque beauties strolled out on stage to start gyrating to the beats the DJ was laying down on the turntables. It was a sight to behold for a kid from the Canadian prairies. In those days, seeing an African-American woman in Edmonton *period* was something of a rarity, but seeing two wearing clothes that barely covered their unmentionables temporarily made me forget that I had just spent the past three hours sweating out all my bodily fluids. Pink tongues wagging, big booties gyrating, fingers tipped with long, recently manicured fake nails cupping their massive, silicone-enhanced breasts, shaking them like maracas. This was pretty much worth the price of admission alone, and the group hadn't even taken the stage yet—they were still backstage tucking into a late catered dinner, likely pierogies prepared lovingly by a small group of Ukrainian *babas*.

Finally, 2 Live Crew sauntered out to the performance area. They greeted the gyrating dancers with a few slaps of the ass, and the crowd, being both relieved and desperate to tell their friends they had seen some actual hip hop in "the City of Champions," let out a thunderous cheer. The whole group was there: Fresh Kid Ice, Brother Marquis, and the group's lead rapper, producer, marketer, and all-around guru, Luther "Luke Skyywalker" Campbell—all of them presumably well fed and ready to perform to the best of their abilities. The opening sample that kicked off "Me So Horny" began to play over the loudspeakers—audio taken from a scene in Stanley Kubrick's *Full Metal Jacket* in which a Vietnamese prostitute propositions an American soldier.

The dancers hopped up on the two massive speakers on either side of the stage and we were off! Campbell was up first, and I was immediately blown away by the accuracy of his rhymes. It was almost as if he was *too* precise. It was almost as if he wasn't rapping at all. It was almost as if he was lip-synching.

And that's because of course he *was* lip-synching.

He was mouthing the words to a recorded track. *Is this how it is at all hip hop concerts?* I asked myself. I tried to pass it off as a group not quite warmed up and ready to perform. Perhaps the next tune would give them a chance to show off their considerable South Florida rhyming skills. Meanwhile the two gyrating dancing girls were distracting us from the fact that we had spent three hours waiting to see four dudes lip-synch. The two girls were definitely earning whatever money they were being paid, bent over directly in front of the stage as Campbell and his cronies took turns playing slap the bongos. Not only had I never seen a booty shake like that, I had never seen a booty like that *ever.* I smiled at my friends, who were equally mesmerized by the display.

After the final beats of "Me So Horny" had played, the entire crowd roared in satisfaction. It was fairly obvious we were being duped here, but everyone was just relieved to be getting some sort of a show instead of slowly dying of thirst. DJ Mr. Mixx dropped the beat on the next track and we were off again. The nasally voiced Fresh Kid Ice had the first verse on this one, but this time he didn't even bother to mouth the words. We could hear the track on the speakers, the dancers were still gyrating to the very best of their abilities, but Fresh Kid Ice just stood there with a goofy look on his face, as if to say: "Whoops! Oh well, we already have your money anyway." Even a group of prairie kids who were just happy to be there had seen enough. A chorus of boos began to rain down on the filth peddlers from South Beach. But rather than become petulant about it, the Crew tightened up their act and finished strong, turning in as good a lip-synch performance as I had seen, leaving it all on the stage, holding nothing back. We had been robbed of our money and time, but we still cheered when the group walked away.

Sensing our impatience, Tone Loc came on immediately after the Crew was done—and he actually performed live, rapping into the microphone and performing awkward, choreographed dance moves that looked like a seniors' underwater aerobics class without the pool. Tone Loc was a big, heavy man, and he truly looked like he was moving in slow motion. The requisite hits were performed satisfactorily, but two neon-bikini-clad dancers were pretty hard to follow. Not to mention that even though most of the people in the crowd probably had Tone Loc's album, few of them had likely listened to it more than once all the way through. By that point, we had also spent five hours standing, dancing, and booing in a space best described as a really, really cheap and disgusting sauna. The night ended mercifully, and my poor father met us outside. I can't imagine how bad we must have smelled as we climbed into the back of his Chevrolet Suburban for the hour-and-a-half journey home.

After that, I didn't listen to much 2 Live Crew anymore. The illusion had been shattered, and the group's popularity quickly waned in the music community. It's not hard to believe now that these lip-synchers weren't considered hip hop pioneers when it was all said and done. Just opportunists.

Not long after that I saw the video for "Smells Like Teen Spirit" for the first time at a hotel while away at a tournament with my high school volleyball team. Suddenly hip hop took a major back-seat to my newest obsession: indie rock. Less lip-synching, fewer gyrating booty dancers, but equal amounts of sweat and thirst.

Chapter 5

The Joke Goes Too Far

It was the summer of 1993, another beautiful sunny day that lasted until 11:30 at night and made us all realize why we loved living in Northern Alberta, and why we tolerated those long, cold winter months. I was working the entire summer in my father's drugstore. Weeknights were mostly spent "swinging the sticks" at the Athabasca Golf and Country Club—something you could do after work because the sun went down so late. Fridays, we would all gather at Loggers Pub at the Best Western Hotel for pitchers of recycled beer and line dancing. Saturdays, you hoped someone was having a party, even a high school party—anything to get out of the house for a few hours.

One weekend a neighbour from university named Jen came to visit, and I was thrilled to find out that my high school classmate Krista Horstemeier was having a house party at her mom's place a few kilometres out of town. Time to show Jen some prairie hospitality!

My friend Robin Bobocel was also back in Athabasca working for his dad. Knowing that a few of us would end up at Krista's house that evening and knowing I would pass by Robin's parents' house on my way to Krista's, I decided to call and see if he wanted me to pick him up in my 1970 Buick Skylark, with its bench seats perfect for carrying loads of people to parties, and also great for the sex I *wasn't* having.

I called Robin's house and there was no answer, so the answering machine picked up. This is where things went horribly awry.

Ever since we were in the seventh grade, my close circle of friends called each other "Joke," short for "Physical Joke," as a reference to all of us being incapable of performing even the simplest physical tasks, as well as not being able to get or maintain an erection. This was absolutely not true, of course. It was the opposite. I actually got too many erections. (*Too Many Erections* was an alternative title for this book.) But it was hilarious to pretend that at the ripe ol' age of thirteen our bodies had already broken down and we were pretty much useless to everyone, especially women. So we all called each other "Joke" for the majority of my junior and senior high school years. A typical conversation with one of my friends would go something like this:

"Joooooke, what's wrong with you? You're pathetic."

"Oh, I know, Joke. I know. My tiny little penis is flaccid and unattractive to women."

"Oh, mine too, Joke, mine too."

It's a real surprise we weren't all getting laid more with this Proust-like dialogue we had going between us each and every school day. The worst part is this dialogue continued right up until high school graduation and beyond. So when I called Robin that fateful Saturday afternoon in the summer of 1993 and got the answering machine, the message I left sounded something like this:

"Joke, it's Joke. Where are you? I'm disappointed in you, Joke. If you don't pick up the phone I'm going to come over there. I'm going to come over to your house and I'm going to body-slam your mother, Edwina. Then when I'm finished with her I'm going to apply the Macho Man elbow off the top rope to your dad, Danny. Then when they are both on the floor I'm going to give them both the Hulk Hogan leg drop. That's right, Joke. They are going to suffer physical pain, and this is all your fault." *Click*.

By then Robin's mom and dad had begrudgingly accepted us calling them by their first names. Hopefully, I thought, they would find the message funny. If they didn't find the message funny, well, what harm could I have really done? They would just think I was kind of a douchebag. And they probably already thought that anyway.

That evening I took Jen to my favourite restaurant in town: Giorgio's Pizza and Steakhouse. Like approximately 72 percent of Italian restaurants on the prairies, this one was owned and operated by a Greek family. George and Helen Skagos worked there every single day with their son Jimmy and daughter Athena, both a couple years my senior. On occasion George, who had a ferocious Greek temper, would blow up at someone working for him in the restaurant, and it made for startling—and fascinating—dinner theatre. You could tell it was coming by the looks on the faces of the waitresses who were not in the family: They would scurry out of the kitchen like something bad was about to happen, and then you would suddenly hear George's thick, Greek-accented voice bellow from the back: "I TOLD YOU SHUT UP! SHUT UP!" We would all look around awkwardly for about a second, then return to the best souvlaki this side of Estevan, Saskatchewan—yet another prairie town where a Greek family runs the Italian restaurant.

After devouring a "Medium Number 3" (pepperoni and cheese),

Jen and I hopped into the Buick and sped down the highway toward Krista's house. I still hadn't heard back from Robin. This being the pre-cellphone days, it was unlikely I'd be able to get in touch with him, so I assumed he would meet us out at the party.

The party was a blast—a classic prairie summer soiree where everyone gathered in the kitchen and talked and drank. There were almost never drugs at these parties, not even marijuana. Just a lot of really cheap vodka like Silent Sam or, worse, Alberta Vodka, and probably more than a few cans of Club Beer, easily the worst brew of its era. About two hours into the party, as Jen and I chatted amiably with some of my former high school classmates who were back home for the summer, Krista came around the corner and walked up to me.

"Phone is for you," she said.

This was *highly* unusual. Again, this is pre-cellphone era, so if someone was actually calling the home of the party you were attending something had to be *seriously* wrong.

My father was, for the most part, a pretty happy guy. He was not a happy guy that evening in summer 1993, however.

"Hello?"

"Jay, it's Dad."

The tone of his voice was *dead serious*.

"Uh, hey, what's going on?" I asked.

He got right to the point. "Did you leave a voice message at the Bobocels' house where you said you would body-slam Robin's mom and hit Robin's dad?"

Well, that wasn't *exactly* right. I believe I said I would deliver a Macho Man flying elbow to Robin's dad, but I wasn't about to argue semantics with the man.

"Yeah, that was me," I said.

"They called the *fucking cops*." My dad rarely cursed, but this was as good a time as any to do it. "They didn't recognize your voice and they thought they were really being threatened. They're at the police station and they're threatening to press charges."

Gulp.

"Get back here *right fucking now.*"

"Oh-kay." I hung up.

Well this was awkward. I mean it was awkward enough that Robin's mom and dad had called the cops and were considering pressing charges, but I also had a guest in town, and a female one at that. I was trying to impress this girl, and nothing says "impress a girl" like having your dad scream at you while you're led into the police station in handcuffs.

We drove back into town. "My dad might be pretty upset. I'm worried about what you might see when we get back," I said, trying to get ahead of the situation. Jen assured me that everything would be fine and that she had been through the same kind of thing before and that everything would be all right.

Really? I thought to myself. This tiny woman had left an inappropriate message on the answering machine of her friend's parents that detailed various decapitating wrestling moves that would cripple said parents? I found this hard to believe, but I wanted to lean over and kiss her for being so sweet and kind and understanding. I would have, but the way my night was going I would likely have lost control of the wheel.

When we arrived back at my family's house there was no one waiting outside. No cops, no vehicles other than our own. At least the neighbours wouldn't see me at my darkest hour. I sheepishly made my way up the front walk, but before I could climb the stairs my dad opened the door and there was pure fire in his eyes.

"Get the *fuck* in here." He honestly didn't swear that often, almost never at all. He was really, really pissed. This was that terrible combination of your son not only screwing up but embarrassing you publicly in the process. All in a tiny little prairie town where everyone knew everything that happened to everyone else. This was not the way he wanted to spend a quiet Saturday evening at home.

We stood in the entryway with my father across from us. I couldn't even look over at Jen at this point I was so mortified. I was about to get called to the carpet by my father in front of a girl from college. Seriously, was there any worse scenario other than a fatal disease?

My dad spoke slowly. "I will tell you one thing right now. I will not hesitate to kick your ass out of this house."

What? That's not the opening line I imagined. Kick me out of this house? For leaving an inappropriate phone message?

"I am fucking serious," he said.

"Hey, I know. I'm sorry." I didn't know what else to say.

He quickly recognized his surroundings and turned to Jen. "I'm very sorry you have to hear this."

"Oh, it's fine," said Jen. It took everything for me not to laugh out loud at this entire exchange, but I knew that might push Dad's rage over the edge.

"We've got to go down to the police station."

Oh, lovely.

After leaving Jen behind at the house, probably wondering if she should try to steal one of the neighbour's cars and make a break for it, Dad and I hopped into his Silverado and drove the two miles to the Athabasca RCMP barracks located right across from the high school. The drive was a short one, but Dad had a few more things to say.

"You guys need to stop calling each other 'Joke.' Quit fucking calling each other that stupid name." He did have a point. Had I

46

identified myself, it's unlikely we would be in this mess. In that case, the Bobocels would simply think I was a little punk and not someone who was about to break into their home and try to kill them using a slow and deliberate display of professional wrestling moves. Instead, I had kept up a weird identification tag for my friends since we were all thirteen years old, and now it was coming back to bite me in the form of criminal charges. Worse yet, I was now eighteen and could be tried as an adult, meaning I might be destined to spend my second year of university doing correspondence courses from jail.

As luck would have it, and because this day might as well get shittier, we pulled up to the police station at the exact same time as the Bobocels. This wasn't going to be uncomfortable at all. Robin's father, Daniel, didn't even say a word, but his mother, Edwina, couldn't hold her tongue.

"This will all be over in a few minutes, guys," she said matter-of-factly. Turns out the Bobocels had been told that it was indeed one of their son's idiot friends who'd made the threatening phone call. Now all that was left was the humiliation.

After Mrs. Bobocel made the comment my dad did something I'd never seen him do to someone in my entire life. He disrespected another adult in front of me. My father was always worried about his reputation because when you're a small-town business owner reputation is everything—unless you sell lottery tickets, in which case you can probably get by without any personality at all. We bought all our vehicles from local car dealerships and shopped at other local stores as much as we could. My parents tried to treat everyone with respect in and outside of their store. So imagine my surprise when after hearing the comment from Mrs. Bobocel that it would all be over in a minute, he snapped back at her, "Yeah, whatever."

It was all I could do to stop myself from laughing. Basically, he was just mad that he'd been dragged into all of this stupidity. Just another summer night on the prairies when you have an idiot for a son. (That was also an alternative title for this book.)

We all walked into the police station and were led into a conference room in the back where two cops were standing with a tape recorder.

I should immediately correct myself and say it was actually one cop and one guy that those of us young people around town who sometimes got into trouble liked to call a rent-a-cop. A rent-a-cop was an auxiliary police officer who would help out the local RCMP detachment from time to time. Basically, he or she was a person who had pledged to spend their free time breaking up fights between drunks at the old Union Hotel bar downtown because, I don't know, they wanted small-town justice? Making matters significantly worse was the fact that the rent-a-cop was a former student at my high school named Glenn whom I had known since we were both about twelve years old. Glenn was only two years my senior, but he had been a rent-a-cop basically since he was eighteen. He probably applied at fourteen, but they held him off until he became an adult. There was to me something very strange about a person who is only twenty years of age and wants to spend their Saturday nights riding in a cop car trying to bust low-level criminal activity in the small town they grew up in. Almost every single case that this person would tackle could involve someone they went to high school with. That's like being a glorified hall monitor. I don't care if Glenn wanted to be a cop or actually even became one. At the age of twenty you should probably be the obnoxious drunk guy at the bar instead of the obnoxious guy who hauls the drunk guy out of there.

Glenn gave me a look of . . . disappointment? He didn't even acknowledge that he knew me. I guess maybe he wasn't allowed to? I sat down next to my dad, with the Bobocels across the table. The cop started the conversation in an effort to get us out of there as quickly as possible, so he could go back to patrolling the streets for drivers who were only coming to rolling stops and not full stops.

"Jay, I'm going to play you this tape, and I need you to tell me if this is your voice on it, okay?" The cop seemed nice. At this point every single person in the room was painfully aware that this was much more embarrassing and humiliating for me than anything resembling real criminal activity.

"Okay," I said, and nodded. I had watched my share of cop shows. I was trying to appear as co-operative as possible, so as to perhaps be given a lesser sentence.

The cop played the tape. I hoped that perhaps my mention of Hulk Hogan leg drops and Macho Man flying elbows and various other wrestling moves might elicit a few chuckles from this some-what sombre crowd. Maybe it would start with Robin's dad, who was always pretty quiet but good for a joke here and there. Then upon seeing Daniel snickering, my dad might start to crack a smile. And then finally Edwina herself, realizing how painfully stupid it was for her to listen to a message that detailed her and her hus-band's decapitation by various wrestling maneuvers and assume that someone in town wanted her and her husband dead, might actually start to burst out laughing and look over at me with a smile that said: "I'm sorry, let's all go for chicken and potato wedges at that gas station by the river that smells like the oil of a thousand chickens and potato wedges." Something romantic and wonderful like that. Then the cops themselves would have no choice but to join in what were now full-scale belly laughs, putting their arms around each other as tears streamed down their cheeks.

Alas, it was not meant to be. The entire room was silent and unre-sponsive each and every time I called Robin "Joke" on the message.

The two boys in blue in the room probably thought this would just be the first of many future visits to their station for various calls involving me and offensive or perhaps eventually dirty phone messages left for the parents of almost every other person I went to high school with. "The old Answering Machine Bandit has struck again," they'd say, as Glenn attached the siren to the top of their Ford LTD and sped off to find and arrest me near the gas station by the river with my mouth full of chicken and potato wedges.

"You understand how serious this is don't you, Jay?" said the real officer as Glenn looked on silently watching, judging, and thinking he was better than me—even though we once played intramural volleyball together and seemed to get along just fine, and even though it seemed painfully obvious to me that he was wandering around this great big world with a giant nightstick shoved very far up his ass.

"Yes, I do. And guys," I turned to the Bobocels, "I'm really sorry. It was supposed to be a funny little message left for Robin and I crossed the line."

The real officer spoke again: "The Bobocels are not going to press charges, Jay, but consider yourself lucky. Issuing threats to another citizen is a serious crime."

"I know, and like I said, I'm very sorry." I was getting no reaction from the Bobocels whatsoever.

After the interrogation was over, we all wandered back to our vehicles silently. Meanwhile, neither my father nor the Bobocels made any effort to say goodbye, and I felt terrible that I had caused some sort of rift between my parents and my friend's parents. Never a good thing, especially in a small town.

We returned to the house, and Jen and I descended to the basement to pour a couple of drinks while I regaled her with brave stories about myself staring down and taking on two members of the Athabasca Phone Message Crimes Division Investigative Squad.

"No matter the pressure, I wouldn't crack," I said to Jen, who was now clearly daydreaming about getting the hell out of there.

I don't exactly remember how the weekend with Jennifer ended, but by the next year she and I would gradually lose touch. She realized her dream of qualifying for medical school, and I eventually abandoned the University of Alberta altogether, taking my life down a different path to broadcasting school in Toronto. I'd like to think the reason we drifted apart was because both of our lives were moving in different directions, but a small part of me assumes that seeing how stupid and juvenile I really was that weekend she came to visit was enough to make her start looking elsewhere for companionship.

She probably made the right decision.

The Monday after the interrogation, I was back working at my father's drugstore. That summer I was the receiver, and while that might be a great jumping off point for a highly inappropriate joke about homosexuality, I can assure you that the only receiving I was doing was several daily orders of diapers, formula, prescription drugs, and magazines. I would get to work before everyone each morning, open up the store, make the coffee, and then pop open the back door and wait for the various delivery trucks to start dropping off the merchandise we had ordered. My dad would arrive not long after and start work in the dispensary. As is typical with my father, he held no grudge toward me for my behaviour that had ruined the previous weekend. We carried on like normal that day as if nothing had ever happened at all.

Then around noon Dad walked outside. I wondered where he was headed because this was highly unusual. He never walked to get his lunch; usually he packed something from home. Curious, I went outside after him and saw that he was walking to meet someone in a pickup truck in the parking lot. The guy got out of the truck, shook my dad's hand, and began talking to him about what seemed like a serious subject.

It was Mr. Bobocel.

The two spoke for a while as I stood at the door watching like an idiot. Finally, they waved me over, and I sheepishly shuffled past the gravel alley behind the store to the paved parking lot and approached them.

"Mr. Bobocel here just wanted to make sure everything was okay between us and them, and of course I told him it was," explained Dad.

"It sure is," I said, then added, "I feel like a real idiot."

"Well, you are," said Mr. Bobocel with a laugh. "But I'm hoping we can forget all of this."

Just the words I wanted to hear. He shook both of our hands again and got back into his truck. After that, I stopped calling my friends "Joke." After that, I stopped leaving phone messages altogether.

Chapter 6

Making Enemies at the Coliseum

Northlands Coliseum
Edmonton, Alberta
October, 1992

"Well, maybe the team would appreciate it if the place didn't feel like a church all the time!" I exclaimed.

"We're trying to enjoy the game! We'll cheer when they score," the lady yelled back at me. She looked to be a bit older than my mom.

"They need more encouragement than that. They're terrible!" I tried to reason with her.

"Oh, why don't you just shut up," she said, exasperated.

"Why don't *you* just shut up," I replied.

What the hell was going on here? Weren't we all supposed to

be cheering for the same team? Yet for some reason it seemed this entire section of the Coliseum had decided I was cheering just a bit *too* enthusiastically. Now everyone around me was alternating between watching the action on the ice and shooting me dirty looks over their shoulders. At some point this evening, I figured there was an ever-increasing chance that someone (perhaps that woman I'd been arguing with) was going to reach across the aisle and slug me. How did it ever come to this?

Growing up in the late '70s and early '80s I was one of those extremely lucky kids whose dad was willing to fork over his hard-earned money for season's tickets to the local NHL team—in my case, the Edmonton Oilers. My dad split them with a couple other guys as there was no way he would have been able to make it to every game while continuing to run his own business. But he and I probably went to ten or so games every year from 1980 to 1990—the most glorious years in the history of the Edmonton Oilers franchise. It was the days of Grant Fuhr, Paul Coffey, Mark Messier, Jari Kurri, Kevin Lowe, and the Great One himself, Wayne Gretzky. Talk about being born and raised in the right place and the right time—and with the right parents.

I remember the weather almost always being terrible—bitter cold and snowy—as we made the hour-and-a-half drive into "the City," though I don't ever remember missing a single game due to the weather. We'd usually try to find a place to park on the front lawn of somebody's house near the Coliseum where a kid would be waiting outside with a flashlight, collecting money and guiding cars to their spots. This is poo-pooed nowadays, but back then it was common practice to line up the cars right next to each other in front of neighbouring houses close to the arena. Dad liked those spots because he believed it allowed him to get out of town quicker. Or maybe he was just cheap. Likely a bit of both.

Once safely parked, we would make our way through the snow and cold to the building alongside other bundled-up Oilers fans wearing their Gretzky, Kurri, Messier, and Fuhr jerseys under winter jackets. The buzz around the Coliseum during those glory years was palpable. We Northern Albertans honestly thought we'd have the best team in the NHL for as long as these guys were playing in the league. Why would coach and general manager Glen Sather ever trade these guys? We had the best team in the world! In Edmonton! Even when Paul Coffey justifiably held out for more money and became the first of the great young Oilers to be traded (to Pittsburgh, for a package that included Craig Simpson, which didn't turn out too bad for the Oilers in the end), there was still no sense that this team would be broken up over an inability to pay their superstars. In those days, there was genuine excitement in the air of the city of Edmonton—dubbed "the city of Champions" after a string of Stanley Cup wins for the Oilers and Grey Cup wins for the Eskimos.

I remember the Oilers doing some elaborate pre-game ceremony for Wayne Gretzky's birthday during the early years where then-owner Peter Pocklington came out with a contract that Wayne signed in front of the entire arena. The contract supposedly kept him with the Oilers until 1999! (Legend has it he didn't actually sign the papers in front of him.) The Oilers were all we talked about at school and at our own little small-town rink. And up until Gretzky got traded it was inconceivable that the Oilers would become some small-market feeder team. Unfortunately, that's exactly what happened after Gretzky left. Mark Messier led them to one more Cup in 1990, but then everything started to fall apart. The stars of the team began to get traded away, and eventually the Oilers were unable to compete with the bigger-market, high-spending teams of the league.

Which brings me to the last year my dad had season's tickets to the Oilers. It was 1992, and I very nearly got myself banned from the Northlands Coliseum altogether.

I was attending the University of Alberta and living in "the City." My dad always kept his tickets at my apartment, so if he couldn't make it in for a game, I'd be welcome to take one of my friends in his place. It was a pretty sweet arrangement, especially for my friends. Naturally, I didn't appreciate my good fortune, and as usual, I managed to embarrass my father completely.

Sometime in October 1992, I attended a game with my roommate and best friend, Trevor Sawatzky. For whatever reason that evening, the fans at the Coliseum got under our skin. We lamented the fact that the crowd was so much quieter than it had been during those wonderful playoff runs leading up to the Oilers' last Stanley Cup in 1990.

I've talked to many people who've gone on road trips through Western Canada to watch their favourite teams face off against the Canucks, Flames, and Oilers, expecting the kind of raucous crowds you'd find in Montreal or Winnipeg. Instead, what they usually find is a decidedly stoic bunch that stay pretty quiet unless it's a playoff situation—and in the case of the Oilers, that hasn't occurred in quite a while.

Back in the '80s, *The Hockey News* published the results of an anonymous survey of NHL players that asked questions including "What's the quietest building in the National Hockey League?" Edmonton's Coliseum and Calgary's Saddledome were at the top of the list. The buildings were the loudest during playoff time, but for the rest of the year it was akin to playing hockey in a well-supervised library. I've always thought Calgary native and former NHL goal-tender, broadcaster, and current Columbus Blue Jackets president John Davidson had the best explanation for this phenomenon. Fans in Edmonton and Calgary, he explained, don't come to games to get loaded, socialize, and scream for their favourite player to score the winning goal. They come to the games to *watch hockey*. They are students of the game and know it better than anyone. They don't need to yell "SHOOT!" every time someone touches the puck on a power play the way Kings fans do whenever I go to games at the Staples Center in downtown Los Angeles. They've watched the sport their entire lives, and they understand every nuance because most of them played the game at some point during their prairie upbringing. They love watching a fight, but it's not the only reason they attend, which may very well be the case in several American markets. Sure, prairie hockey fans love to socialize as much as anyone in North America, but when the game is on they're *watching* not talking. And that means the buildings can get eerily quiet. It all makes perfect sense to me now.

That said, I simply cannot defend the great fans of the Oilers, Flames, and Canucks for staying quiet and contemplative when the home team scores a goal!

I can remember many a late night in Toronto when I'd be sitting in my old leather chair watching the second half of a *Hockey Night in Canada* double-header on the CBC featuring the Oilers, and the second Edmonton scored a goal the camera would scan the crowd at the Coliseum to gauge their reaction. And every single game it'd be the same: Although many fans in the crowd would be stand-ing and cheering, there'd be just as many (if not more) inexplicably sitting down with their hands tucked underneath their legs and a look on their faces that screamed boredom. I mean, I understand that you've paid your hard-earned money to get into the building and you can react to your home team's scoring any way you like, but for God's sake if your team scores you should be required to stand up at the very least. Stand up and clap. Maybe even let out a "woo."

So there I am with Trevor at the Coliseum in the fall of 1992, and the Edmonton crowd is being typically quiet. Frustrated, we decided to take it upon ourselves to liven them up a bit. So we started cheering. *Loudly.* We weren't using foul language or anything—we were just yelling really loud, telling Shjon Podein to hurry up and finish his check and Kelly Buchberger to drop the gloves. Giving it to the referees a bit. Throwing in a few "LET'S GO OILERS" chants. Not surprisingly, it wasn't long before we started to draw the attention of the other fans in our section. A few people asked Trevor and me to "quiet down" so they could "watch the game." Many others just shot us angry looks. Soon, the polite requests turned into angry shouting. In typical Onrait fashion, I didn't back down from these requests to keep it down, suggesting instead that everyone in my section needed to wake up a little bit.

I still maintain I was absolutely in the right. I was *cheering loudly for the home team.* Most pro sports teams would encourage this. They would *expect* it, even. But not in Edmonton.

I suppose the quiet atmosphere in the Coliseum that evening got to me, and I ended up making a few new enemies in our section. Still, there were no physical confrontations or anything, and we left the game that evening without any real incident. In fact, I didn't give the night a second thought until two days later when my dad called me at home from his drugstore in Athabasca.

"Hey, Jay, were you a little loud at the Oilers game the other night?" he asked.

"I dunno. I guess, maybe," I replied.

"Maybe a little *too* loud?" he continued.

"Maybe a little. Why?"

"I just got a call from Bill Tuele."

Bill Tuele—the director of public relations for the Oilers. This wasn't quite as exciting as the last phone call my dad received from the Edmonton Oilers front office. That time, it'd been legendary Oilers tough guy Dave Semenko—the most famous of the Oiler tough guys, the man responsible for protecting Wayne Gretzky during the early years of the Great One's career. Dave was now working for the Oilers in a ticketing capacity, calling up season's ticket holders and encouraging them to renew. One can only imagine the team's strategy: Who the hell would say no when Dave Semenko asked for money?

Mr. Tuele called my dad to tell him there had been twelve separate complaints to the team's PR department about a "tall, loud, lanky, and obnoxious young man" who'd been disturbing everyone and preventing them from enjoying the game. *Twelve separate complaints!* Mr. Tuele wasn't threatening to take my dad's tickets away or anything, he just thought my father might like to know that the person using them had alienated pretty much every single person around him and that he might want to think twice about who he gave his tickets to the next time.

"Mr. Tuele gave me his number," explained my dad. "I suggest you get on the phone with him *now* and apologize." It wasn't really a suggestion.

"Got it," I replied sheepishly.

Mr. Tuele was actually very gracious. "I appreciate the fact that you called, Jay," he said. "We just want to make sure that everyone who comes to our games can have an enjoyable time."

I wished I could've asked Mr. Tuele to join me in our section for a game sometime. I'm not sure if he would have seen *everyone* enjoying themselves.

Dad punished me by taking back the rest of the year's tickets; and he decided not to renew them the following year. Soon after, I moved to Ontario to begin my career in broadcasting, but I watched with great interest when the Oilers made their surprise run to the Stanley Cup Final in 2006. Sadly, they lost in a heartbreaking seven games to the Carolina Hurricanes. On the bright side, though, watching from across the country I could see—anyone could see—that the atmosphere in the Oilers' arena was absolutely incredible.

On one particularly memorable night, as the Edmonton crowd sang "O Canada" at full volume, led by longtime Oilers dressing room attendant and local legend Joey Moss, the camera focused on NHL commissioner Gary Bettman. The look on his face said it all. He simply could not believe that an NHL building could be so loud. It could be that way every night if we wanted it to be.

Chapter 7

Christmas at MuchMusic

Back in my days at Ryerson, in my second year of radio and television arts, I took an English class alongside a kind and beautiful student named Monita Rajpal. Monita was one of those focused and driven students who had *it*, and you just knew she was going to succeed in the industry one day. She went on to read the news for CityTV's CP24 Cable news channel, which led to a job overseas at CNN International, where she works today as one of the lead anchors for the worldwide news network out of their Hong Kong bureau. I love the rare times that I get to check in to an overseas hotel, flip on the television in my room, and see Monita, having not aged a single day, deliver the news in between episodes of *Amanpour* and *Parts Unknown with Anthony Bourdain*. It's always nice to see good, hard-working people succeed just as you hoped they would.

Back in second year, however, Monita was just a student like me who would take any volunteer gig that she thought could make a difference after graduation. At that time, Monita was volunteering in the CityTV newsroom, likely fetching coffee and making copies. Then, one fateful day in December of 1995, she was tasked with recruiting other students to serve as unpaid waiters for the CityTV/MuchMusic Christmas party—a party that took place on the top floor of a bar called Montana at the corner of Richmond and John streets, right behind the City/Much building. I had zero experience as a waiter or bartender, but I was willing to take pretty much any volunteer gig offered to me. So, one Friday night I put on a pair of black trousers and a white shirt that I had ironed in my dorm room and walked to Montana for my first and only job in the hospitality industry.

A very nice but stressed-out woman was put in charge of the volunteers, and upon gathering us together when we arrived she set out to determine which of these ragtag students actually had any serving experience. I obviously had none, so they quickly decided that I would man the door and take entry tickets. This meant I would be the first person to greet such City/Much luminaries as Gord Martineau, Anne Mroczkowski, Ben Chin, and Steve Anthony—a longtime Much VJ whom I became friends with just before my time working in Toronto ended. Steve was a mile-a-minute talker with a terrific broadcast voice. Nowadays, Steve plies his trade as co-host of the CP24 breakfast show. His most notorious recent incident happened in late 2013 when, while reporting live from the Rogers Centre on an upcoming Monster Truck event, he made the inexplicable snap decision to perform a running drop kick on one of the massive tires on the Monster Truck in the background. You can actually hear his bones crack in the clip. Steve suffered a broken hip that required surgery. Every time I talk to him on the phone I just listen because I can never get a word in edgewise.

That evening back at Christmas 1996, however, Steve didn't differentiate me from the twenty-five other broadcast students on hand all trying to make valuable contacts while handing out drinks. And frankly, if I were him I would have paid more attention to the girls anyway.

Finally, after pretty much everyone else had arrived, the king-pin, City/Much boss Moses Znaimer, strolled in. He had his sister and CityTV reporter Libby on one arm and *Fashion Television* host Jeanne Beker on the other. It was a little bit like watching Hugh Hefner arrive at a party thrown at the Playboy Mansion, except instead of twenty-one-year-old surgically enhanced nude models, he was strolling in with his most trusted lieutenants. I wandered inside to help out in any way I could, mostly just making small talk and trying to flirt with Monita. After Mr. Znaimer arrived, it was time for the show—unfortunately not a band called in from his contacts at MuchMusic, which was a missed opportunity really. (I like to imagine it would have been someone cool from the early days of Canadian music video prosperity, maybe Platinum Blonde, Honeymoon Suite, or Maestro Fresh Wes—the possibilities are frankly endless). Instead, the show involved a yearly ritual utilizing the resources the network had already set in place, namely Speakers' Corner.

Speakers' Corner was a small video booth, just slightly larger than a standard telephone booth, that had been installed on the corner of the City/Much building. The idea for the booth came from its namesake in old London where Londoners could park themselves on a crate in Hyde Park and air their grievances about the current state of the British government (and the monarchy too, within reason). The original spot exists to this day, and I remember the digital team from Fox using it for a story they put together during the London Olympics when they had no rights to shoot any actual Olympic footage in the venues and had to improvise (something Dan and I would become very familiar with at the Sochi Games in 2014).

The City/Much Speakers' Corner was a more updated version, featuring a camera that accepted one dollar coins for charity. Insert that loonie and you had exactly one minute to say whatever was on your mind. Unhappy with the current government? Job prospects for young people in the country? The Toronto Maple Leafs? This was your chance to have your say. It became a very popular tourist attraction and was actually turned into its own television show that aired Friday nights on CityTV. Innovative and cheap Canadian content.

About half an hour after Znaimer arrived on the scene, we were instructed to place chairs in front of a big screen that was being set up at the front of the room for some sort of presentation. The very front row was to consist of only three chairs: one each for Mr. Znaimer, Ms. Znaimer, and Ms. Beker. Once everyone had taken their places there was a palpable buzz in the air. Everyone here clearly knew something very interesting was about to happen, except for the volunteers—who were about to get a major shock.

I discovered that evening in December 1996 that the camera in the Speakers' Corner booth was active *at all times*, not just when you inserted your loonie. Everything that was said or happened in that booth on the corner of Queen and John streets in downtown Toronto was recorded for posterity. *Everything.*

The projector turned on and a title graphic appeared on the screen that said "The Best of Speakers' Corner: City/Much Christmas Party Edition." This could be fun, I thought. I was ready to hear clip after clip of hilarious would-be comedians going off about issues in their life using language too obscene for television. Turns out I was selling the whole operation a bit short. There weren't really any rants to be seen, other than the occasional homeless person who had decided to sleep in the booth for the night and wasn't happy about the smell in the tiny confined space. For the most part "The Best of Speakers' Corner" featured a plethora of unspeakable sex acts in a tiny, confined, and rather filthy booth.

There was no subtle way to edit these clips together. The video started with a male and female making out in the booth and then a quick cut to that same female pulling out the male's penis and going down on him. She then looked to the camera and gave a wink, which led to a rousing cheer from the crowd. We were just getting started. A quick cut to a drunken frat boy whipping out his wang and pissing all over the seat in the booth, marking his territory if you will. This led to another quick cut back to the original couple. This time the woman was on top of the man and full-on penetration could be seen as clear as day. We were being treated to (*very*) amateur pornography for Christmas. On and on it went. A woman facing directly into the camera with a giant grin on her face as she was clearly being plowed from behind by some dude in the middle of a cold, dark Toronto night. More blow jobs, some women on men, some men on men, all of them met with cheers from the crowd.

The filth just continued on from there. Even more blow jobs, more fucking, more homeless dudes and frat boys pissing. I was actually a little surprised there wasn't a clip of someone shitting. I wondered to myself if the booth had a hose hookup right next to it so it could be sprayed down every morning. Finally, the video came to an end and the screen flashed "Happy Holidays" with a picture of Ed the Sock next to it, leading to a massive cheer from the gathered employees—a job well done for another year. I was still in a state of shock. City/Much had a reputation for being the bad boys of Canadian broadcasting, but I did not walk into the company's holiday gathering thinking we would be sitting around watching dirty movies like a bunch of thirteen-year-olds who had just discovered the parental control password on their parents' cable system. Maybe this was just a company that liked to film themselves?

A few years later, when I had just returned to TSN and the concept of viral videos had begun to take shape, the company's star news anchor, Gord Martineau, was featured in a video that had been posted online, likely by a disgruntled ex-CityTV employee. In the clip, Martineau stands next to fellow longtime City anchor Anne Mroczkowski and repeatedly grabs his nuts between takes of a news update.

"I've got your news right here!" he jokes.

It was clearly all in good fun and no one in the video seemed offended whatsoever, but it definitely stripped the stately newsman façade from Martineau in my eyes, for better or for worse. Later, in the same leaked video, longtime man-on-the-street reporter Jojo Chintoh can be seen in a Toronto home waiting for an interview subject who was upstairs getting ready for the day. While he waits, the camera follows Chintoh as he snoops around the home a bit—nothing too unusual or scandalous. The problem comes when Chintoh spots the family liquor cabinet and wanting a little morning pick-me-up proceeds to twist the top off a bottle of Baileys and put a sizeable portion into his Tim Hortons coffee cup.

This was the first viral video news scandal I can remember, and it didn't result in any of the offending parties getting fired, but it did serve as a reminder that as long as your microphone is on and a camera is pointed toward you, you have to really watch what you say and do in this industry. And you have to treat people well, especially the people responsible for editing the holiday filth reel.

Chapter 8

Road Trip

When I arrived in Saskatoon in the fall of 1999 for my first job at Global Television, I felt ill-prepared for the task at hand. On-air presentation? I was barely adequate. Luckily, I hosted my first show on a Saturday afternoon when the only people watching were a bunch of seniors gathered around a television set in an extended-care home. The first broadcast went well enough, the second even better, and from there I got into a decent rhythm.

As sports director, I was expected to run a department that included three additional people: my co-anchor on *Sportsline*, our weekend solo anchor, and an intern from a broadcasting school, who would likely do as many interviews and file as many reports as anyone because, hey, it's Canadian TV and free labour was what made it all work. All three individuals in these roles were older than me and yet somehow I was expected to supervise them. I'd barely gotten my feet wet in the industry and already I was required to correct writing mistakes, assign stories, and tell guys when I thought their on-air performance was lacking—even though I was clearly no expert. It was something I was never completely comfortable with, but the guys in the department were so laid back they made it easier. I mentioned Derek Bidwell, my co-anchor on *Sportsline*, in *Anchorboy*, and R.J. Broadhead, who was the weekend anchor. Both guys were easy to get along with and true professionals (Bidwell is laughing reading this because no one in his life has ever called him a true professional). I didn't socialize with either of them too much, however, because I didn't think it was my place. I quickly realized how difficult it was to be a young boss with colleagues your own age or older—people you would normally hang around with but who were suddenly off-limits because you had crossed over to management. This is especially true of interns, who are supposed to be learning from you and taking guidance. But for whatever reason I hit it off with our intern that year in Saskatoon, and it had nothing to do with his looks—which are hideous.

Reid Wilkins was born just a few months before me in 1974 and grew up much like I did in a small Alberta town about an hour from Edmonton called Evansberg. Reid's dad was principal at the local school, and the family lived on an acreage about ten minutes outside of town. He was the school valedictorian, so obviously much smarter than I was, but he also loved sci-fi and comics and all the things I liked. Like me, Reid went to the University of Alberta after high school, but unlike me he actually completed his degree. Then, while working at an Edmonton Blockbuster Video, he decided his lifelong love of the Edmonton Eskimos, Montreal Canadiens, and Montreal Expos was a great reason to dive into the broadcasting business. He enrolled in the Northern Alberta Institute of Technology School of Broadcasting and a year later successfully nabbed an internship at my station, just a few months after I arrived.

We hit it off right away, often spending afternoons in the office doing a rather diabolical Chris Cuthbert impression where Cuthbert, one of our favourite broadcasters, had actually turned into a violent sociopath and was now verbally abusing his colour commentator John Davidson in the broadcast booth. Cuthbert's voice always had to be very high pitched to exaggerate the slightly higher octave his voice took while calling the CFL or NHL.

CHRIS: Well, JD, it looks like the Leafs' defence is easy to penetrate, just as your home will be easy for me to penetrate when I invade it tonight and steal all of your possessions!

JD: Chris, why are you saying this? Why are you saying this on-air to me? This is totally unprofessional!

CHRIS: J . . . D . . . you disappoint me.

This could go on and on for hours. I would be in tears most afternoons talking about Cuthbert the psycho and John Davidson, the sad mensch who had to sit there and take his abuse. People around us trying to work in the newsroom would often shoot us looks like: "What the hell is wrong with you two?" But hey, we were on a roll!

After a year in Saskatoon I made my way to Winnipeg to host a morning breakfast show, while Reid stayed behind to finish his internship and eventually land a job as a sportscaster in Lloydminster, Alberta—or Lloydminster, Saskatchewan, depending on how you looked at the map. "Canada's Border City" was split pretty much down the middle by two provincial lines, and their small CBC station saw many future broadcasting stars pass through on their way to bigger things. Reid was thrilled to get the job, and I was thrilled for him.

About six years later, both of our fortunes had changed, and not necessarily for the better.

I had just walked out on my first wife and triggered a divorce. Things had been bad between us for some time, and I just couldn't go on living like a miserable jerk all the time. So I found an apartment in Toronto's Kensington Market and filled it with my friends' old IKEA Poang chairs so I had something to sit on. Job-wise things were great. After a couple of years working together at TSN, Dan and I were really hitting our stride as an anchor team. Great things were in the cards professionally, but my personal life was a complete shit show. I was making way more than my wife, and I knew I was about to take a major financial kick to the balls. Aside from that, I was depressed about the end of my marriage. My parents have been happily married almost their whole lives, and I struggled to understand why I couldn't get things to work out with my own marriage. We had been so happy at the beginning, but then we moved to Toronto and everything changed. After the separation, I started seeing other women, which for most guys would have been enough to cheer them up, but I was still down in the dumps and needed a pick-me-up.

Meanwhile, Reid was doing even worse. The initial joy and excitement of getting that first job in Lloydminster had worn off, and that's because Reid was *still* there. By now he was running the sports department at CBC Lloydminster, but with all due respect to the good folks who have made Canada's Border City their home, most young broadcasters working at that station soon moved on to greener pastures. For whatever reason, though, this was not the case for my friend Reid. He had applied for several jobs, only to fall just short each and every time. Reid was tired of living in Lloydminster, missing his friends and family back in Edmonton. He was also beginning to wonder if he really had a future in the broadcast business, or if he should just use his outstanding intellect for greater monetary gain somewhere else.

These two similar dips in our life trajectories got us to talking on the phone one day. We both had some vacation time banked, and we had always talked about doing a classic baseball road trip—driving from stadium to stadium, watching game after game, drinking tons of beers, and eating way too many hotdogs for any healthy human. Now that I was no longer married, I was free to hit the open road with my buddy, so we planned the trip for early in the 2007 season.

We decided to concentrate the trip on the East Coast. There were so many potential trips we could have done in the Midwest and out West—Wrigley Field in Chicago beckoned, as did the beautiful and much lauded Pac Bell Park in San Francisco. But we only had a week and we wanted to take in the maximum number of ballparks possible. Besides, by sticking to the East Coast, we would also be able to hit the two most famous sports halls of fame in America: the Baseball Hall of Fame in Cooperstown, New York, and the Pro Football Hall of Fame in Canton, Ohio, just outside of Cleveland.

DAY ONE

To get from game to game, we decided on my 2005 Nissan X-Trail, a vehicle that my wife liked to call a "soccer-Mom car." "Any vehicle that comes in champagne should not be driven by a man," she said. Mine was black, but it still wasn't very cool. Still, it was a comfortable ride and it had a six-disc CD changer, which was still somewhat revolutionary in the days before MP3s and then streaming took over and changed the way we listened to music. We actually brought CDs on the trip. We decided to allow ourselves five each, taking into account that we were possibly trying to introduce each other to some new bands.

One of the things that used to make me laugh the most about

Reid when I first met him back in Saskatoon was his unabashed love of the English hair-metal titans Def Leppard. Growing up as we did in the '80s, Leppard was just about the biggest band in the entire world. Their first album, *High 'n' Dry*, made them stars, their second, *Pyromania*, made them bigger stars. And then they took a long hiatus following a tragic accident in which drummer Rick Allen lost an arm, then learned to drum again while in hospital using a revolutionary computer foot-pedal system. Once Rick had the technique down, they went back into the studio and recorded their third album, *Hysteria*, which made them total megastars. The album ended up being one of the biggest sellers of all time and spawned a myriad of hit singles that dominated rock *and* Top 40 radio throughout 1989. Everyone, and I mean everyone, was into Def Leppard that year. They filled stadiums around the world multiple times over. Then they took another unexplained four-year hiatus before returning with *Euphoria* in 1993, featuring perhaps the worst follow-up single to a megaselling album ever, "Let's Get Rocked." As I heard the song and watched the horrible computer-animated video for the first time at the young age of nineteen, I just knew it. "It's over," I told myself. They were done being a megaband and would continue on for the next couple of decades as a nostalgia act, alongside groups like Kiss, Poison, and Cinderella.

But Reid had taken an entirely different view. While I was listening to Radiohead's *OK Computer* and Fatboy Slim's *You've Come a Long Way, Baby* in 1999, Reid was acting like the past ten years had never happened—for him, Leppard was still on top of the music world. He waited for every new Leppard effort like he was a thirteen-year-old waiting for the Backstreet Boys to release their new chart topper. I thought he was joking at first, pretending to be into such an unfashionable band simply to be ironic, but he was *absolutely serious* about his love for Def Leppard.

So when Reid showed up for our road trip, I wasn't at all surprised that he'd made sure to bring *Vault: Def Leppard Greatest Hits*, along with a few other staples of classic rock, like *Van Halen's Greatest Hits*, and a future classic, *Queens of the Stone Age*. I predictably gravitated toward indie rock that I hoped might pique his interest in some newer music, though in the end the album of mine he ended up liking the best was Weezer's *Pinkerton*, an initially maligned follow-up to the band's debut album that effectively ended their careers before becoming a classic in hindsight and reviving the band's fortunes years later.

With our CDs loaded in the six-disc changer, we were ready to hit the open road. We crossed the border at Niagara Falls, drove through Buffalo as fast as humanly possibly (sorry, Buffalo), and began to make our way east toward Cooperstown for our first stop: the Baseball Hall of Fame.

I honestly don't know what I was expecting when we pulled into Cooperstown on a surprisingly poorly marked road that afternoon. I guess I was picturing a charming little town in the middle of upstate New York with a beautiful shrine to America's Pastime. For the most part that's what I got, though I couldn't quite believe how different baseball's approach was compared with hockey. Hockey historians have famously argued about the birthplace of Canada's favourite game. Did the first stick and puck action take place in the Maritimes? Ontario? Quebec? It seemed the easiest and most logical solution to situate the Hockey Hall of Fame in neutral territory—Toronto's downtown—where it has thrived for the most part in an old bank building close to the Air Canada Centre, home of the Maple Leafs. Cooperstown has history on its side, because *all* baseball historians acknowledge it as the birthplace of the sport.

The town is literally centred around the Hall of Fame—and pretty much nothing else. There is really nothing else to do there. The entire town is even more remote than you might expect. But the Hall was really spectacular and set up beautifully.

The thing I remember most distinctly was the newest display in the Hall at that time: Curt Schilling's bloody sock. Schilling, a talented veteran pitcher who had joined the Boston Red Sox as Boston attempted to finally break the Curse of the Bambino and win their first World Series in eighty-six years, had torn a tendon in his right ankle earlier in the 2004 post-season. In any other situation a pitcher with such an injury would be out of the lineup for a while, but Schilling refused to sit, and after having doctors suture his torn tendon he took the mound in Game Six of the American League Championship Series in one of the most memorable relief-pitching appearances in history. The Fox TV cameras kept cutting to Schilling's ankle just above his right cleat where blood appeared to be leaking out and staining his sock. The Red Sox went on to win the ALCS after being down 3-0 to the Yankees and then went on to the World Series against the St. Louis Cardinals, where the same scenario repeated itself for the cameras as the gutsy veteran Schilling started Game Two.

Legend had it that the ALCS bloody sock was thrown in the trash at Yankee Stadium, but the World Series Game Two bloody sock was immediately donated to the Baseball Hall of Fame after Boston won the World Series and finally exorcised their demons. Our visit to Cooperstown was just a couple of years after that happened so the whole scenario was still fresh in our minds, and everyone who visited the Hall that day gathered around the glass case to admire the sock. Pretty hilarious to think about all of us gathering around a display case to admire a sock, but that's what makes the Hall so great: real baseball fans gathering together to see little pieces of history in person.

Sadly, not even ten years later in 2014, Schilling was broke—the victim of some bad investments—and decided to auction off the sock to pay his creditors. I suppose we were lucky to see that bloody rag when we did. When the sock did sell it went for almost a hundred grand! A little piece of baseball history gone to the highest bidder, and we had been there to see it.

DAY TWO

After catching an afternoon game at old Yankee Stadium, in which Sammy Sosa finished up his career as a designated hitter for the Texas Rangers, we hopped on the subway from the Bronx and rode downtown to Katz's Deli in the Lower East Side. Old Yankee Stadium had history but not a ton of charm. Normally, I hate to see old buildings torn down, but in the case of Yankee Stadium, it made perfect sense to me. I would have led the charge to have it torn down. It was just old and worn out, and somehow it didn't age as well as other old baseball stadiums. After the new stadium was built across the street, I returned to see it a few years later and was surprised by the negative reaction it had received. Yes, it was massive—probably *too* massive—but I loved the façade on the outside as you walked up to the stadium. To me, it felt historic the first time I saw it, like something that would age really, really well.

On our way into Manhattan, Reid confessed to me that he felt he'd hit a wall in the business and wasn't sure he could continue the way he was going. Reid was an Alberta boy through and through, and he loved covering the Alberta Junior Hockey League in which Lloydminster had a successful franchise, but living in the town was proving tiresome for him. It was a small town built around oil and agriculture, not too far removed from the town he grew up in, but there just wasn't anything there to offer him joy in his off-hours anymore. It wasn't as if he had ambitions to move to Toronto or New York or Los Angeles. He just wanted to return to Edmonton, where a guy who was into comic books and Def Leppard might find a little more to make him happy.

Beyond that, though, his frustration was with the nature of our business itself. Reid knew more about sports than I ever would, and he'd learned more about the teams in his small market than anyone before him. You simply could not find a more prepared, diligent, and hard-working guy. He was completely easy to get along with. He had applied for job after job after job, but each and every time he came up short, often to younger broadcasters who were working for *him*. With each "no" he became understandably more and more dejected. I couldn't deny how unfair the whole process was. The bottom line was that Reid didn't have conventional TV good looks and no one wanted to take a chance on him. The visual medium had thrown a wall up in his face and now, after putting years of his life into the business, he was starting to wonder if the whole thing was a fruitless exercise.

I felt a little sheepish listening to him. Clearly the only reason I had moved up faster than Reid was that I had looks that were *just* good enough for television and enough charm to let me bluff through the rest. It certainly wasn't knowledge, because when it came to sports, Reid had me beaten hands down. Why should it be this way? Why should I have succeeded while he got left behind? All along, I had told him to continue fighting the good fight—to keep applying for jobs when I knew he probably wasn't going to get them. Now, listening to him break down on the subway, I changed my position. I told him to quit.

"Just go back to Lloydminster and quit. You'll be a helluva lot happier."

That piece of advice went against everything I used to believe in.

Quitting was easy; sticking it out was the hard part. I was always a big believer in paying your dues in this business and embracing the steps it took to get to the market you wanted to work in. But in my mind Reid had done all he could as an on-air television sports broadcaster; it was time to move on.

DAY THREE

The next day we drove to Boston for two games at Fenway Park. Fenway had been refurbished instead of replaced when pretty much the entire city protested after the Red Sox announced they wanted to build a new park in 1999. It's hard to imagine a more spectacular place to cheer on your home team—no wonder Boston fans have remained so loyal to their proud franchise, even during those lean years. *This* was a baseball stadium. Bench seating behind home plate that looked very similar to a small-town Alberta hockey rink? Yep. Terrible hotdogs wrapped in what appeared to be slices of white bread? Flat-out classics as far as everyone in Beantown was concerned. Then there was the history of the place: the Green Monster, Pesky's Pole, the manual scoreboard out in left field. All of it lived up to the enormous hype as I walked into the place just off of Yawkey Way. We saw two games there, a Sunday game and then a Mother's Day matinee.

The Mother's Day matinee was truly memorable. Jeremy Guthrie was pitching a *gem* for the Orioles that afternoon and Baltimore was comfortably in control all the way until the bottom of the ninth inning. Guthrie was a rookie at the time and was doing magical work on the mound. In the bottom of the ninth, after getting the first out, the Red Sox hit a pop-up near home plate and the Orioles catcher missed it, allowing Boston to get a runner on base. No worries, we thought. Guthrie had thrown a ridiculously low number of pitches, something like eighty-three in total. The base runner clearly wasn't his fault, so there was no need to take him out. But they *did* take him out. And after watching the Orioles reliever get the first out, thinking Baltimore would get out of the inning and pick up the win, the Red Sox suddenly started hitting everything. All this despite the fact that they had taken Manny Ramirez, arguably their best hitter, out of the game. The Red Sox scored six runs in the ninth and came back to win 6-5, sending everyone home with a slightly drunken smile on their face. Amazing what a six-run comeback will do for a baseball-crazy city.

It was 2007, the year they won the World Series.

We hit the town that night and had a great time—or so I thought. In a cab on the way back to our hotel, Reid suddenly wasn't feeling so good. Was it the clam chowder? The wine? Truth be told, it was probably the vodka shots, or better yet a combination of all three. Either way, we were almost home free when Reid began to vocalize a serious issue with his stomach and then actually start puking.

Puking in the backseat of the cab. All over the floor.

We were on a freeway so we couldn't open the door, and it came on too suddenly for him to get the cabbie to pull over. The driver was understandably furious with us, yelling and screaming from the front of the cab while weaving in his lane. "I'm sorry! I'm sorry!" Reid choked out as he opened the window and tried to vomit outside while we were moving fifty miles an hour, his spittle hitting the back of the cab. I felt bad for him, but at the same time I was a little frustrated. How could he have not known he wasn't feeling good? Couldn't he have said something earlier? Maybe we could have pulled off into a residential area where at least we could have found a place for him to puke on the street. I was embarrassed. Reid was never a partier, but this seemed almost childish. I was suddenly filled with regret about the whole trip for reasons I couldn't really explain. Maybe I hadn't spent enough time with the guy, and maybe I should have before agreeing to this, because we still had five more days on the road together.

DAY FOUR

The next day we stopped in Baltimore to see the Orioles play at Camden Yards, the first of the new "old school" stadiums. It was completed a couple years after Toronto's SkyDome and effectively rendered that stadium outdated just three years after it was built. Camden Yards was a true modern classic, but the team was a mess in 2007 and the park was barely full. It seemed such a shame. Although I did appreciate getting to sample Boog's Barbeque—a stand on Eutaw Street behind the right-field bleachers owned by legendary Orioles first baseman Boog Powell. Now this was great ballpark food! Orioles fans may have been treated to some pretty bad baseball during that time, but at least the barbeque somewhat made up for it.

From there it was on to Pittsburgh, but we decided to do the trip over two days, stopping halfway in Wilkes-Barre, Pennsylvania. All due respect to the good folks of Wilkes-Barre, but we didn't find a lot of action in town on a Monday night. We did find a twenty-four-hour Costco, however, where we bought beer and Reid picked up some apple juice. I had never travelled with a grown man who drank apple juice every morning. It was another thing about him that annoyed me. Couldn't he drink orange juice like a normal adult? Was he stuck in suspended adolescence?

DAY FIVE

The next morning we woke early to grab a quick breakfast in the hotel diner before getting on the road to Pittsburgh for the Pirates game that evening. I ordered pancakes and orange juice. Reid ordered *cereal* and *apple juice*. I tried to hide my annoyance at his choices as I scarfed down my flapjacks. Besides, soon we'd be back on the road.

I started behind the wheel. I'd been doing most of the driving on the trip since we had taken my car. I think we were listening to "So This Is Love?" by Van Halen when disaster struck. I started to feel my stomach gurgling—that familiar feeling that my lower intestines were in serious distress and I desperately needed to find a toilet. What the hell happened, I wondered? It's not like I ate a ton of breakfast potatoes with garlic, onions, and hot peppers. I had pancakes, for Christ's sake! Reid continued to chatter away in the passenger seat while I muttered "yes" and "no" answers, all the while concentrating on not filling my pants.

We came upon a massive truck stop about an hour outside of Wilkes-Barre, and I pulled over and went inside. It was the type of mammoth complex that features five or six restaurants, close to fifty gas pumps, and hundreds of shitters. Thankfully, the men's restroom was lined with about a hundred stalls to handle all the truckers, families, and highway travellers who needed to put their waste somewhere on their long journeys.

PNC Park in Pittsburgh had recently beaten out the much more hyped AT&T Park (at the time called Pac Bell Park) in San Francisco in an ESPN poll of the most beautiful baseball stadiums in the country. People had been absolutely *raving* about it, so we were understandably pretty excited to see it. There was absolutely no way I was going to let some stupid stomach bug keep me from going to a game later that evening. But whatever was making me sick was relentless and simply would not stop.

A gas station restroom is pretty much the closest thing to hell on earth, and on that dreary afternoon I was the devil. I just destroyed that toilet, and when I was done destroying that toilet I didn't exactly feel much better. I had nothing left to shit out, but I also knew anything I ate from that point on would immediately go in one end and out the other. Not to mention the fact that my stomach *still* wasn't right. I was filled with rage. How the hell could this happen to me now? Was it the heavens punishing me for not being more sympathetic to Reid when he got sick in the cab back in Boston? It sure felt that way.

Meanwhile, Reid had gassed up the soccer-Mom car, paid the bill, and was now sitting in the front seat starting to worry about me. He actually wandered back toward the men's restroom just as I was coming out, and I was so full of rage and anger and in so much pain I just walked past him and said, "Let's get out of here." As we walked toward the car, we passed a family of four heading inside for lunch. Out of the corner of my eye, I saw a four- or five-foot-tall garbage can with flaps on either side. All of the anger over the fact that I was starting to realize my chances of attending this baseball game were becoming slimmer and slimmer by the second made me do something I will forever regret.

Just as the family of four walked past, I yelled "SHIT!" and karate-kicked the garbage can like I was Daniel LaRusso in *The Karate Kid Part III*, knocking it over and spilling its dirty contents on the ground. The whole incident was over in a split second, and I was instantly embarrassed and a little shocked by what I had done. I turned around to see the family staring at me, the father grabbing his children by the shoulders and leading them away from the monster I had become.

"Sorry!" I yelled out to no avail. Reid just turned away and started walking toward the car in silence. So much for the jovial bonding session that we'd planned back in Toronto.

After a couple more hours in the car, during which I lay across the backseat in agony while Reid put the pedal to the metal with Weezer cranked to full blast, trying to get us to Pittsburgh as soon as possible so he could finally separate himself from me and my bowels, we finally made it to the outskirts of the city. The whole time we were driving I stared at the ceiling of the vehicle trying to figure out what the hell was causing me to feel this way. And then it hit me.

It was the Goddamned orange juice.

Suddenly, all those glasses of apple juice were starting to look pretty good.

The OJ was just too acidic for my sensitive stomach, and it was wreaking havoc in a way that nothing had ever done before.

The highway we were on was thankfully not that busy, and Reid was in an understandably strange state—unsure of the road, with its many tunnels. As I felt sicker and sicker in the back, and as I discovered the culprit of my peril, I got more and more vocal: "Fucking orange juice. Fucking orange juice . . ." I kept muttering as Reid turned up the volume on *Pinkerton*. "If I ever go back to Wilkes-Barre, I'm going to find the chef from that hotel and kick him right in the nuts." Reid felt helpless. He was such a people pleaser and there was nothing he could do. I was making him more uncomfortable than any acidic beverage could ever make me. I consoled myself with the knowledge that this long nightmare of a drive would soon be over.

*

Instead of GPS or a navigation system, we had literally printed out dozens of Google maps, so one of us would have to navigate while the other drove. This was just a bit before GPS systems were commonplace on smart phones. Our system had been working quite well until I went and consumed too much acidic morning beverage and destroyed my insides. Now Reid was forced to drive *and* navigate through a city he had never set foot in. Our hotel was at Exit 4. I was in the back becoming more and more uncomfortable and subsequently more and more belligerent. "Why haven't we made it yet? Are we there yet? I'm about to paint the back of this car with my poop if you don't drive faster."

Reid would respond, frantic, both hands gripping the wheel: "We're getting there, man. I haven't been to Pittsburgh before!" In other words, the usual conversation between two dudes on a baseball road trip. The exit numbers were descending from high to low as we approached downtown, and therefore Reid deduced that we were on the right track. I continued to be a belligerent asshole in the backseat.

"That chef is a dead man . . . that chef is a dead man . . ."

Reid kept his eyes on the exit signs.

We passed Exit 7.

We passed Exit 5.

We passed Exit 3.

Reid looked back, his face painted with agony. "I don't know what to tell you, Jay. I think we missed Exit 4."

"You son of a bitch!" I said. "I'm dying back here!"

We hit Exit 2. Then we went into a tunnel. "Jay, I'm going to have to double back and try to find it."

I wasn't even listening by this point. How was I going to hold on? I was just daydreaming about toilets—toilets with big comfy seats. Remember the ones at your grandmother's house with the squishy, comfortable seats and the soft shaggy rug covers for the lid? I wanted to embrace one of those toilets at that moment. I wanted to hug it like it was my long-lost child—a baby I had given up for adoption that was now in my arms and ready for me to sit and shit on. Granted, that's kind of a strange baby/parent relationship, but don't judge my parenting techniques. I was a desperate man. Tears were literally beginning to stream down my face.

Then suddenly, we emerged from the tunnel. And there it was. *Exit 4.*

It didn't matter how completely messed up the Pittsburgh interstate exit system was in our minds; what mattered was that the second Reid pulled onto the Exit 4 off-ramp, he saw the hotel.

"I see it!" he proclaimed, a man so very happy at the thought that he'd soon get away from my company.

He wheeled into the entrance of the hotel and parked as close to the lobby as he could, and I sprinted inside with the speed of an escaped convict who'd just had the spotlight shone on him during a midnight jailbreak. There was a public restroom in the lobby, and I made that public restroom my bitch for the next ten minutes while Reid checked in. We met back at the car.

"We have to move the car," I said.

"Why?" asked Reid, who was probably seconds away from hitting a man in a violent rage for the first time in his entire life.

"Because when we pulled up I was in such a rush to empty my bowels that I put a dent in this car next to us."

We both looked at the door of the car next to us. The dent was *huge.*

"Let's move the car," said Reid.

By the time we got to our rooms, my bowels were once again

calling out for a toilet. I decided to skip the toilet altogether this time and just go for the tub. As George Costanza once said, "It's all pipes!"

While I was continuing to deposit every remaining ounce of waste in my body into the plumbing of that roadside hotel, Reid went downstairs to the business centre to check his email. He'd been waiting on some news about a job. One of the sportscasters at CTV Edmonton was going on maternity leave and there was a fill-in job up for grabs. Despite the uncertainty over where it would lead after the year was up, Reid was more determined than ever to get that job. And once again, he was easily the most qualified person for it.

After about fifteen minutes of hanging my ass over the edge of the tub, I heard a light knock on the door of my room. I said, "Just a second!" and washed up before answering it. A dejected Reid entered the room. Amazingly, he did not pass out from the smell in the bathroom. He just stood in front of the television set.

"I didn't get the job in Edmonton."

"Oh." I wasn't expecting that. "I'm sorry, man."

"And I quit my job in Lloydminster."

Wow!

"I'm just done. I called my old boss and gave him my two weeks' notice." He was practically in tears.

In years past I would have tried to talk him out of it, to tell him to stick things out at least until he found something—anything—else. Then I remembered what I had said on the subway. It was time to move on. The decision had already been made. The strange thing was that as conservative as I usually was about these things, I thought he had made the right decision and I had given him the right advice.

"CTV Edmonton gave the job to my weekend guy," he explained.

Now I *really* thought he had made the right decision.

At some point, we all come to grips with the fact that television is a visual medium, and often the best and most talented journalists and broadcasters don't catch their big breaks. Reid wasn't as handsome as his younger, much less experienced and less qualified weekend guy. He'd literally taught that weekend guy everything he knew about the business, but the weekend guy probably looked like a frat boy, and *that's* what news directors wanted in their sports anchor.

When people ask me how they should put together a demo tape, I think back to the advice I was given by a news director some years ago: Begin with a montage of you, just you, doing on-camera reads. Stand-ups, at the news desk, whatever. Basically you're giving the news director a chance to decide if he or she likes the *look* of you. Before that news director ever has a chance to determine how good a journalist you are, they need to determine if their audience will actually want to turn on their television and look at you every night. If the answer is "no" then sadly no amount of journalistic expertise is going to land you that job.

There is a terrific sports anchor who has worked at Global Television Vancouver (formerly BCTV) for years named Squire Barnes. He is funny, he's sharp, and his delivery is understated and unique. Squire is a truly different personality and has become extremely popular in the market. He also looks like the kind of guy who would dress up in costume to attend the San Diego Comic Con. In other words, he's not your typical sportscaster. But somewhere along the line someone took a chance on Squire and it worked. Reid never got that chance, never had a person in a position of power like Squire and I had who believed in him.

*

Meanwhile, back in Pittsburgh, I had to excuse myself and return to the bathroom. I sat on the toilet this time like a normal person, or as normal as I could pretend to be given the situation. Reid detailed his new, hastily constructed life plan to me through the bathroom door, competing with my loud and violent shits, which he ignored as if I were his family dog. He would sell his place in Lloydminster and return to Edmonton. He would take some more time off and then try to figure out where he wanted life to take him.

"Good for you, buddy!" I said, before letting out a loud PFFFFFFFFFFFFFTTTTTT from the bathroom.

After about ten minutes of discussion and pooping, Reid checked his watch and realized he had to go if he was going to make the start of the Pirates game.

"Fuck it, I'm coming with you!" I said.

I didn't care how sick I was. I wasn't going to leave my buddy alone while he was downtrodden and trying to figure out the next step of his life. Reid had bravely driven me across the state of Pennsylvania while I was belligerent, verbally abusive to him, and suffering from a violent stomach bug. The least I could do was suck it up and make sure he wasn't alone that night.

So I turned on the water in the tub and scrubbed my ass one last time—if I had a Brillo pad I probably would have run it up and down the crack just to make sure I got everything. Then a quick change of clothes and we were off to PNC Park. The park truly was the highlight of the trip—perhaps the most perfect ballpark I had ever seen. Smaller than most of the other parks we had visited, at around 35,000 seats—about the size of Fenway—but the layout was spectacular. Same with the food and the view of the Roberto Clemente Bridge, perfectly situated just beyond the outfield. We somehow ran into Devin Steigerwald, son of Pittsburgh Penguins play-by-play announcer Paul Steigerwald, and he talked about the years of frustration Bucs fans had been forced to suffer through since Barry Bonds, Bobby Bonilla, and Jim Leyland had left town in the early 1990s. We had a terrific time.

My one regret is that I didn't get a chance to eat one of the famous Primanti Brothers sandwiches—the family had a location in the park and they were apparently a must-try. My stomach, while finally starting to feel a bit better, just wasn't quite up to the task.

DAY SIX

The next day we drove to Cleveland and in the course of one day miraculously saw the Pro Football Hall of Fame, the Rock and Roll Hall of Fame, and a Cleveland Indians game at Jacobs Field against the Minnesota Twins—all before driving the six hours back to Toronto. To say I would like to return to have a longer visit to "the Cleve" would be an understatement. The Pro Football Hall of Fame was great but admittedly a bit underwhelming compared with its baseball counterpart. The Rock and Roll Hall of Fame was a mind-blower. I was engrossed in a display about handwritten lyrics by Sting for the Police when I suddenly realized the place was closing and I hadn't even seen half of it. Someday I will drag my kids there and force them to stand and listen as I explain why it was fashionable for Elvis to wear bedazzled jumpsuits on stage.

When we got home, Reid followed through on his promise to quit his job and move back to Edmonton. Not long after that he got a job as a news producer with A-Channel and then returned to his true love, sports, as the host of *Inside Sports* and the pre- and post-game shows on Edmonton Oilers broadcasts for 630 CHED, a station I had grown up listening to when it was a Top 40 juggernaut. Now CHED is an all-news-and-talk station, and they have the radio rights to broadcast the Oilers and Edmonton Eskimos games from the NHL and CFL. Reid finally found someone who believed in him, and every once in a while he'll call me up and I'll appear on his show. We don't break out the sociopathic Chris Cuthbert impersonations anymore, but we do discuss our ill-fated baseball trip on occasion. It was a life changer for both of us in so many ways. Reid learned that he had to take a different path to get what he wanted. I learned to never again touch a glass of orange juice.

Chapter 9

Some Time in New York City

My first trip to New York City was back in 1996—a nine-hour bus ride with a few dozen Ryerson students from the radio and television arts program. In those days, New York was still in its pre-Giuliani cleanup mode and Times Square was still a porny wasteland neon dump. We went to legendary Lower East Side music venue CBGB, where the likes of the Talking Heads, Blondie, and the Ramones had all hit it big, but the experience was lost on most of my fellow classmates, who couldn't figure out why we were going to a run-down dive bar in the Bowery instead of a "cool" club like the Limelight. I also dragged a group of friends to Dangerfield's Comedy Club all the way out in Queens because I knew that was where Andrew Dice Clay had recorded his *The Day the Laughter Died* comedy album. Blissfully unaware of New York City's geography at the time, we all piled into a cab from Manhattan instead of riding on the subway. The comics were okay, but they would probably have been just as good if we'd gone to Carolines in Times Square. After that experience, and the overpriced drinks at Dangerfield's, I was never allowed to plan another outing in New York ever again.

A couple years later, my best friend, Peter Sayn-Wittgenstein, was offered the use of an Upper West Side apartment for the weekend and invited me along for a trip. On the flight down I read a *Details* magazine, back when people actually read magazines. I was captivated by an article about Michael Alig, a notorious "club kid" on New York's nightlife scene and a close associate of Canadian-born Manhattan club owner Peter Gatien. The article went into great detail about the fact that Alig had maybe, possibly, chopped up and killed his drug dealer "Angel" in a drug-induced haze, stored him in his bathtub for several days, and then dumped him in the Hudson River. Eventually, Alig was convicted of the crime and sent to jail, but at that point, he was still living freely in New York City, even though pretty much everyone assumed he was guilty.

Our first evening in New York, Peter and I decided to try to be social, so we made our way down to the Bowery Bar, which at the time was one of the hottest nightspots in all of Manhattan. It was located not far from CBGB in an area on the verge of gentrification after years of being a dangerous part of the city. We walked toward the door with absolutely no hope of getting past the massive bouncer since we were two dudes wearing T-shirts with Corn Pops boxes on the front, as well as baggy, unwashed cargo pants.

Suddenly, I spotted Michael Alig wandering toward the club with a group of underage boys trailing behind, who all looked like they'd just arrived off the bus from Iowa. In an uncharacteristically bold move, I approached the club kid:

"Is your name Michael?" (*Brilliant* opening line, Onrait.)

"Yesss," he answered with understandable reluctance.

"Alig?"

"Yesss," he answered again, wondering what the hell I wanted.

"Can we get in here with you?" I asked, fully aware that I was likely about to enter NYC's hottest club with a man who was capable of chopping me into pieces and storing me in his bathtub for a few days.

"Uh, okay," said Alig. And like that, we were in! *We were just cute enough for a killer!* (That was also an alternative title for this book.)

Once through the door, Alig and his merry band of underage boy toys disappeared. But he had provided our passport to Manhattan debauchery, and later that evening I passed out drunk on a small table in the club and was asked to leave.

These days, when Chobi and I visit New York City we are less concerned about which clubs we're going to hit than making sure we get into the best restaurants of the moment. It's time I made a horrifying confession: My wife and I are foodies. That's right, the dreaded "f" word. We've spent many nights bonding over our mutual love of celebrity chefs, overhyped restaurants lit exclusively with Edison bulbs and furnished with reclaimed wood, and the Food Network. Our television-watching schedule breaks down like this: fifty percent sports networks, forty percent Food Network, and ten percent premium cable. I make no apologies for being a foodie. It's fun! However, the foodie movement of the early 2000s brought along with it a frustrating, if understandable, trend: the "no reservation policy" restaurant.

In an effort to keep every seat full, while creating the illusion of demand, many restaurants—including our favourite Toronto restaurant Pizzeria Libretto—simply did not accept reservations, operating instead on a first come, first served basis. This way, no seat ever goes empty and there's always a lineup at the door, or more likely a crowd uncomfortably sandwiched into a small bar at the entryway, awkwardly holding drinks elbow high while simultaneously giving the stink-eye to patrons lingering over their desserts and coffee. Waiting in restaurants like this always gives me flashbacks to that 2 Live Crew concert in Edmonton. But if the food's good enough, I'm willing to play along.

The Spotted Pig in New York is the epitome of another cringe-inducing modern food movement, the gastropub. The concept, of course, involves taking the humble place around the corner where everyone knows your name and elevating the food options beyond ploughman's lunch and chicken wings. In the case of the Pig, they brought in some real culinary heavy hitters. Mario Batali, the venerable Italian-American chef, seemed to be nothing more than an investor/consultant, but adding his name to any restaurant always lends cachet. The head chef, English-born April Bloomfield, has made a name for herself elevating versions of English Pub classics. But perhaps the most interesting investor at the Pig is New York hip hop icon Jay-Z, aka Jay-Hova, Shawn Carter, the new king of New York, Beyoncé's lesser half, and the subject of elevator beatdowns by disgruntled sisters-in-law. The Pig, with all of its faux historical interiors and rich mahogany wood, couldn't be further from the Brooklyn projects where Jay-Z grew up. The place has been raved about online and on television, and it also happens to be in one of the nicest parts of Manhattan's West Village, about as "idyllic New York" as it gets.

So when Chobi and I visited New York together in 2008, it was an obvious choice for at least one of our two dinners that weekend, but we had to be prepared to wait, and wait, and wait. Word was, the wait to get a table at The Spotted Pig could often stretch past the two-hour mark. Luckily, like many no-reservation restaurants, the Pig allows you to leave a phone number with the hostess, so you can roam around the neighbourhood freely and they'll text you when your table is ready, rather than jam yourselves into their tiny entrance and be miserable for two hours.

Our wait that evening wasn't two hours—maybe one at the most—and we were in a great mood when we were summoned back to the restaurant while wandering those leafy and beautiful West Village streets. A smiling hostess led us upstairs to the second floor, past a beautiful central bar and into a room at the back. There we were led directly into a corner booth with a view of the entire restaurant. The table seemed too good for a pair of tourists from Canada, but maybe this was simply all that was available. Either way, we certainly weren't complaining.

Our waiter for the evening was a Bill Hader type, if Bill Hader hadn't made it as a comedian and instead channelled all his comedic energy into a serving job. He was frantic, but kind and helpful in selecting beers from the tap. We ordered as many dishes as we could and they were all truly fantastic: fluffy, Batali-inspired gnocchi and a gorgonzola-laced burger that was easily one of the best I've ever eaten. About ten minutes into the meal I noticed a familiar face at the table directly across from us—David Schwimmer, Ross on *Friends*. He was dressed a lot like his character on *Friends*: khakis and a shirt topped off with a fedora. He was accompanied by his fiancée and they sat quietly chatting at a corner booth, various well-wishers from the restaurant occasionally stopping by for hugs. Ross was likely a neighbourhood regular and who could blame him? If I had a nice apartment in the area I would probably eat at the Pig twice a week.

Suddenly, faux Bill Hader appeared in front of us in a panic. His demeanor had completely changed from friendly and entertaining to "when the hell are you two going to be finished and get the hell out of here!"

"How much longer do you think you guys are going to be?" he asked.

Yes, the dessert is just delicious. Thanks for asking, I thought to myself. What happened to the jovial guy who was treating our dinner like a one-man show? Why did his attitude switch so fast? He scrambled away without explanation. Was Schwimmer upset that I was silently judging his hat? What the hell was going on?

Then, just a few feet away from our table, I noticed a figure staring in our direction. He was African-American, about six feet tall, and very thin. He wore a crisp, fresh-out-of-the-package white T-shirt and baggy black jeans, with a long, red string of rosary beads dangling from his neck and hanging between his chest and navel. He also wore a Yankees cap.

It was Jay-Z, and we were sitting at his table.

Faux Bill Hader re-emerged with a proposition as Jay-Z continued to stare over his shoulder: Would we consider moving to another table in the restaurant? This was just as we were finishing up our meal, a pretty confusing request for any restaurant patron no matter how hot the establishment or who was waiting for your table. He offered no explanation for the request, obviously feeling that Mr. Carter's stare was all the explanation needed.

"We'll be out of your way as soon as you bring us the cheque," I said. That was still not quick enough for Faux Bill Hader, or very likely Jay-Z, but there was really very little that they could do. They asked us to leave and we were leaving. It still didn't change the fact that the gnocchi were frigging delicious.

Then, seconds later, I felt really important, because Jay-Z sat down right next to me.

"Hi," I began.

As I said before, I've always been pretty good with opening lines.

"Hey, guys," said Jay-Z. "Sorry about this. We would be happy to move you to that table right across the room. I just have a big group coming in."

"It's really no trouble at all. We were just heading out," I replied. This was really happening. We were having a casual conversation with Jay-Z as we were both trying to pretend he wasn't kicking us out of his table at his restaurant, all while David Schwimmer and his fiancée sat directly across from us and pretended not to notice.

At that point Jay-Z's entire entourage walked into the room. It was pretty much exactly as you would expect. Despite the fact that Mr. Carter was now happily married to Ms. Beyoncé Knowles, she was nowhere to be found. Instead, the requisite models were along for the party that night. Two girls sat on one side of Jay-Z and the other two sat on the other side of my wife. Each and every one of the models was obviously thrilled that they were one entire Canadian mixed-race couple away from the person whose attention they were trying to capture that evening. One of Jay-Z's buddies then squeezed himself in between Chobi and the models and briefly tried to make small talk with the future Mrs. Onrait: "You guys in town for a while, err . . ." Another one of Jay-Z's buddies sat on the far end of the other models who were seated next to Mr. Carter. Pudgy, wearing sunglasses, and just happy to be there, we later dubbed him "Jay-Z's weed-rolling buddy" because he was clearly the "Turtle" of Mr. Carter's entourage. Jay-Z made some small talk with the models as I signed my credit card receipt, with a frantic Faux Bill Hader waiting to snatch it out of my hand like a golden ticket to freedom. We started to get up to leave when Mr. Carter spoke:

"Would you like to have a shot of Patron with us?"

I froze.

For a split second I thought back to my one and only visit to Peter Luger Steakhouse in Williamsburg, Brooklyn. Established long before Williamsburg became the hipster haven it is today, Peter Luger was a must-stop for steak lovers in New York City, serving arguably the best porterhouse in America. The place was bare bones wood décor, accepted only cash, and featured old, grizzled male waiters who had all likely worked there since they graduated high school. I had been warned about those waiters and their impatience with patrons who were unsure about what they wanted to order. There was really only one thing to order at Peter Luger, the porterhouse steak. I had even been told a story about patrons getting ridiculed by the waiters when they dared to order a seafood dish. A friend of mine attended a bachelor party dinner there with seven other guys, and they all sat back in shock as their waiter dictated the meal they were about to eat: "You want some steaks, guys? Some spinach? Some potatoes? Good." None of them got a word in. They also said it didn't matter because the food was so delicious they would have taken any abuse handed to them for the right to watch those old, grizzled veteran servers delicately tip their platter full of meat to one side and scoop up the juices to pour all over their protein. When I finally visited the restaurant with Chobi, I warned her about the possible poor treatment we were about to receive. We were led to our table, and I sat in my seat and had just picked up my menu when a server appeared in front of us.

"You guys ready?" he asked.

"I literally just picked up the menu," I replied.

"What's the problem?" he said.

What's the problem?

Who the hell was this guy? I was a patron in his restaurant! What happened to treating the customers with respect? Of course, I didn't actually say this to the guy. Instead, I just sat there, mouth agape, totally stumped for a reply, while Chobi jumped in: "We'll take the steak for two, spinach, fried potatoes, and a bottle of red wine."

"Great," said the waiter, and off he went to terrorize another group of tourists.

Flashback to Jay-Z asking "Would you like to have a shot of Patron with us?" and once again I was completely dumbfounded. There was probably drool hanging down my lip, and he probably thought I was some sort of sad invalid. Thankfully, once again my wife jumped in to save the day:

"Sure! We'd love a shot of Patron!" she exclaimed.

Done. Just like that, Faux Bill Hader was dispatched to the bar to grab Patron shots for us, Jay-Z, the chatty buddy, the weed-rolling buddy, and the four models. As you can imagine, Faux Hader was a little frazzled, having thought he was rid of us, only to have his boss prolong this somewhat awkward encounter.

A minute or so later FBH returned with a tray of shots, handed them out to everyone, and scurried off.

"Cheers. Thanks for your understanding, guys," said Jay-Z.

"Thanks for having us!" I said. *What? That didn't make sense.* Oh well.

I poured the icy, almost frozen alcohol down my throat. I love tequila but don't know much about the subtleties of it so I can't tell you which Patron we were drinking that evening, but I can tell you that if Patron makes a brand of tequila that is distilled from the tears of royal children then this must have been it. It was the smoothest, most delicious shot of tequila ever, and then it was gone.

Just as we were expected to be.

"Thanks, man," I said and shook his hand as we got up to leave.

The next day my wife was reading People.com and she saw a

paparazzi pic of Jay-Z strolling through a heavily touristed part of Soho hand-in-hand with Beyoncé. The picture had been taken just hours before our encounter. I guess after an afternoon of shopping with the missus he decided to call up his buddies and told them to bring along some models. Shopping in Soho with all those tourists must have been too much for him to take. Then the poor guy shows up at *his* restaurant to find that Faux Bill Hader had given away his favourite table to the two most obvious tourists in New York City.

I will always appreciate how kindly he kicked our asses out of there.

Chapter 10

Medicine

Chobi and I moved to California in the summer of 2013. The good people at Fox were kind enough to put us up in a condo right by the water in Santa Monica while we looked for a permanent place to live. It was paradise. Just steps from our front door was the beach, the ocean, the sun! But as much as I loved walking along the beach strip, I realized pretty quickly that if I was going to survive in Los Angeles, I was going to have to drive. Everywhere. And that meant getting a California state driver's licence from the dreaded DMV.

Long before I arrived in Santa Monica, I had heard the horror stories of the California Department of Motor Vehicles—the massive, slow-moving lineups and general inefficiency are the stuff of legend. Luckily for me, because Fox was trying so hard to show their appreciation for Dan and me coming all the way to the USA, we had been assigned relocation experts to assist with the move. Fox Sports' ultra kingpin David Hill even sent us each an email when we agreed to the job. Hill himself had immigrated to Los

Angeles from his native Australia, and he assured us that our assigned relocation experts would make the entire move smooth and easy. He was absolutely correct. My wife and I were assigned a wonderful lady from Redondo Beach named Susan Graven, who booked every DMV appointment for me and then showed up to meet me on my appointment days and waited until my appointments were over, just like my mom. It was a luxury for someone so disorganized, and an absolute necessity. How did other people move to the United States without a dedicated relocation expert to take care of booking their appointments to get a Social Security Card? If talented Canadians over the years had known how difficult a move this was without a mother figure holding one's hand, we might not have seen the likes of Alan Thicke, Martin Short, and Robert Goulet making their way down to SoCal to find success with audiences south of the border.

Having been a driver for almost thirty years (we get our learner's permit at age fourteen in Alberta, unless you grow up on a farm, in which case you're likely already driving around age six or seven), I was somewhat taken aback when I learned that I would have to take an actual driver's test to obtain my California licence. Suddenly, I began experiencing feelings of terror. What if I failed the driver's test? I was almost forty years old! I hadn't taken a test in years, but clearly past exam experiences had stayed with me because anytime I had a nightmare it was the same scenario: I had reached the end of my four years at Ryerson University, but just before I was about to graduate I was called into the guidance counsellor's office. Turns out I hadn't completed sufficient credits to earn my degree and I was going to have to take classes during the summer. Then I wake up in a holy, sweaty terror with a feeling of relief that can only be described as borderline orgasmic. I hated taking tests when I was young, and I hated the idea of taking one now even more.

Susan herself was a terrible driver, perhaps one of the worst I've ever seen. She had the basics down but fell into the classic talking-too-much-and-not-paying-enough-attention-to-the-road trap that so many of us, including me, fall into. But she managed to meet me at the DMV on the morning of my driver's exam—an exam that inexplicably included both written *and* practical portions. I somehow aced the written exam, despite feeling absolutely terrified about having to sit down and put pencil to paper on an actual test, and I was feeling pretty good about myself until I wheeled my newly-arrived-from-Toronto-via-cross-country-train car into the testing area and a large, silent heavyset man approached. We got into the car and immediately the guy started giving me instructions:

"Turn on your left signal, then your right, now the hazards. Why are you nervous? Don't be nervous."

I wasn't nervous, but this guy was making me nervous. He was like a bully, or a bouncer; this was his chance to lord his power over me in the only setting he could control. I instantly hated this man and I was certain he was going to fail me. We eventually pulled out of the DMV parking lot, and what followed for the next half hour was a series of right turns.

"Turn right here," followed by twenty seconds of silence.

"Turn right here," then another silent twenty seconds of driving in a straight line. "Another right." I hoped I'd never have to do anything behind the wheel in California but circle the block because that was all I was being tested on that day.

Finally, the big burly bully gave me what I thought was going to be a challenge. "Pull up to that curb on the right," he said.

The dreaded parallel parking test. I actually considered myself a brilliant parallel parker and looked forward to proving it to this socially awkward, lumbering oaf. I pulled a car-width from the curb and looked over my shoulder in preparation of backing in to the curb when the bully spoke, enraged: "I didn't ask you to parallel park! I asked you to pull up to the curb!" There were no other cars parked on the side of the road. Even my wife who had never driven a car in her life could have managed this. Was this some kind of a joke?

Ten minutes of more right turns later we were back at the DMV. The bully told me to park and then got out of my car without a word. Did I pass? Fail? There was absolutely no indication. I followed fifteen steps behind him and walked in the front door toward the woman who had handed me my written test an hour before. She told me to stand three steps to the left on a mark on the floor so she could take my picture.

"So you're saying I passed?"

"Yes, didn't he tell you?"

"He did not."

"He can be like that."

Should he still be working here, then? I wondered. No matter, I would never have to see him again, and I was now officially a licensed driver in the great state of California.

A few weeks after my ordeal at the DMV, I was lounging around my beachfront pad, watching a terrific series called *The Layover* on the Travel Channel. This was the second series to be hosted by chef and author Anthony Bourdain after his breakthrough TV hit *No Reservations*. *The Layover* featured a very simple premise: Bourdain would travel to a major metropolis somewhere around the globe and spend approximately thirty-six hours eating, drinking, and lodging at the best places the city had to offer, all the while showing you how you could do the very same. As someone who loved to take such trips, I waited for each episode eagerly. The Los Angeles episode was no exception. Bourdain spent one evening having dinner at super-popular restaurant Animal on Fairfax Avenue with the establishment's co-owners, Jon Shook and Vinny Dotolo. During the course of their conversation the subject of marijuana came up, and Bourdain casually inquired what he would need in order to get his medical marijuana card in the Golden State.

"You need a California driver's licence," replied Shook and Dotolo in unison.

I sat up immediately, the words slowly sinking into my brain. *Hold on*, I thought, *I've got one of those. I've got a California driver's licence!* I figured I had to try to get my card, not because I was going to become a regular user, but just to see if I could. I wanted to know if Jon Shook and Vinny Dotolo were right. And just think of the story this would make! Besides, what's the worst that could possibly happen?

Chobi, of course, wanted no part of this ridiculous adventure. So, like all men who need to do things their wives don't approve of, I waited until she was out of town. She went to visit her mother in Ontario for four days not long after, which gave me plenty of time to research and track down the best and most reputable doctor I could find. Instead, I spent three days in my underwear watching television. Then, on the last day before she was scheduled to return, I panicked after realizing that if I was really going to make this happen, I needed to get it taken care of fast. There was only one destination I had in mind, and that was the shady Venice Beach strip that I'd visited a few years before.

For those of you who've read my first book, *Anchorboy*, you may recall my writing about a press junket I attended for the movie *Blades of Glory* that was so stressful that I sought out recreational drugs on Venice Beach for relief. While walking along the crazy and eclectic Venice Beach strip with its cheap T-shirt stores, art stands, and head shops that day, I stumbled upon something I had never seen before: men and women in their early twenties, dressed in electric green hospital scrubs, amiably corralling tourists into their oceanfront offices to get medical marijuana cards.

Now, I know what you're thinking: *Weren't those "offices" just dressed-up tourist traps? And with a little effort and research, couldn't you have found yourself a much safer and cheaper option?* The answer was a resounding "yes" on both counts. But, as had been a pattern for much of my life, I tend to take the easy way out, which is often the more expensive way. I could wander down to the beach, grab some lunch from one of the food trucks, and then casually enter one of the many "doctor's" offices with all the other tourists, who wouldn't even notice I was there anyway. Besides, it said $40 on the big marijuana leaf outside the office—how much cheaper could a card be than that?

So I made my way down to Venice Beach that warm fall day in November and walked into the first doctor's office I could find. I was a little disappointed that the neon green hospital scrubs crew weren't on duty; instead, only one person was working at a small desk in the corner of what looked like an actual doctor's waiting room. The only difference was that this doctor's office was open to a beachfront walk that featured a lot of fascinating smells: sweat, barbeque, patchouli, weed, ass—you name it, the smell was there in the stifling heat that fall afternoon. The doctor's office did not smell like weed; it just smelled like an old building that hadn't been cleaned in decades.

I approached the young girl at the desk, probably mid-twenties, who was dressed in hospital scrubs that were actually neon blue. She gave me a series of forms to fill out and asked for a photocopy of my driver's licence. There was no turning back now; they were going to have a copy of actual government identification that I had been issued just a week prior. I tried not to think of what they could do with that newly issued government ID as I sat down in the waiting area next to a very young skateboarding couple— the girl at least ten times hotter than the guy—and another older woman my mom's age who said she was from Denver and asked me if she would be able to qualify for a card with a Colorado driver's licence. I apologized for not having the answer and wondered why she would even bother since Colorado had just voted to become the first state to fully legalize the sale and purchase of marijuana for recreational use. Following a nice exchange with the lady, I looked down at my sheets of paper on a clipboard and began filling them out.

Normally, Chobi fills out all forms in our household, and before you chastise me for being lazy I will point out that she does it because she loves it. During my speech at our wedding, I specifically praised the "inexplicable joy she gets out of filling out forms" to knowing laughter from her family and friends. But she was not here to help me now. I was going to have to do this on my own.

Turns out I wasn't there on my own.

Shockingly, this particular operation wanted to make it very easy for you to obtain your "green" card. So easy in fact that they refused to even leave it up to chance. Under the question "For what medical reason do you feel the need to obtain a medical marijuana card?" instead of a few blank lines where one could possibly bullshit their way into a corner like they were writing a high school English exam, the sheet listed ten possible ailments with a box to check beside each of them. In other words, there was literally no wrong answer. "All you have to do is check one, you idiot," the sheet of paper seemed to be saying. So I checked one:

insomnia. As a kid I suffered from crippling insomnia and as an adult it had never really subsided, but nowadays I just chalked it up to the massive can of Yerba Mate I drank at work every evening ("made from the naturally caffeinated leaves of the celebrated South American rainforest holly tree"), as opposed to any minor or major existing medical condition. Nonetheless, "insomnia" seemed like a perfectly legitimate answer, whether it was presented to the doctor I was about to see or to the authorities who could potentially have me deported.

After filling out the rest of the forms with as little information as I possibly could, I was told to wait a little longer because the doctor had not yet arrived. I pictured a nice hippie type—maybe he'd had a private practice for a few years in Brentwood and then decided to cash out and become a beach bum while doling out weed cards in between catching surf breaks. Or perhaps it was a younger, just-out-of-med-school guy who had walked the straight and narrow all his life and now, explicitly defying his traditional Jewish parents, he had become a convert to all the good pot can do for the body and soul and had begun dispensing cards for the one drug his parents couldn't tell their friends about. It was the perfect act of rebellion. I was genuinely curious who might be on the other side of that rather shabby looking wooden door to the doctor's office.

"Jay, the doctor will see you now," said the girl at the front desk. Rather dour and serious for someone working reception at a medical marijuana establishment, I thought.

I took a few steps toward that wood door, the paint peeling and chipping away after years of contact with salty ocean air. I opened it up, expecting to see lava lamps and psychedelic posters on the walls, and instead I saw nothing. Absolutely nothing. There was a large desk and chair, and that was it. They both looked second-hand. There was wood panelling on the walls from the 1970s like the kind in the den of the Brady Bunch house. There were no medical charts or posters, not even a diploma on the wall. Was I being set up? Was I on a reality show? *To Catch a Pothead*?

And just like that, without warning, the doctor entered the room.

He might have been eighty. He might have been *ninety*. He was definitely well past retirement age and had probably come back to work here because the money was just too good to pass up. He was about five-foot-seven, with grey, thinning hair, and wore glasses that would not have been out of place on Bubbles from *Trailer Park Boys*. Thick, round, and plastic, they were more like magnifying glasses, and his eyes were so huge behind them I thought for a second he might be a Muppet. He wore a sports jacket made of heavy wool, with patches on the elbows, like a professor who had just landed his first postgraduate teaching job at a Midwestern college and was trying to look the part. Then there were the pants. In my brief time in Los Angeles I had never seen a single person wear corduroy pants, not even in the deepest hipster pockets of Highland Park and Los Feliz. The weather was simply too warm for such a thick and durable garment. This did not deter this particular doctor, however, who was wearing perhaps the thickest pair of corduroys I had ever seen in my life. I could only imagine how sweaty his undercarriage must have been. His shoes were black and chunky, and he walked with a cane. The whole look screamed: "I'm not from these parts."

I was in temporary shock when he opened his mouth to speak.

"Hi," he said plainly. He didn't bother to ask me my name. He likely didn't bother to ask anyone's name. This was an assembly line and the work needed to be completed quickly.

He walked around me as I sat in the room's only other chair directly across from the empty desk. He walked—slowly—around the desk and with a heavy sigh collapsed into his chair and looked up at me. The whole process likely took as much as forty seconds.

"So, you would like to begin receiving medicine?" he asked. The dour girl at the front desk had corrected me when I had called it "medical marijuana."

"We call it *medicine* around here. This is a doctor's office," she'd said.

Right, right, I thought. *Wink, wink.* I got it. I could play along. No problem.

"Yes, I would like to begin receiving *medicine*. New to the state, just moved here." I had no idea what I was saying. I was really, truly awful at small talk—always have been. Why was I so nervous? I paid forty hard-earned dollars to sit here! I was fidgeting in my seat, and in the sweltering office I was beginning to sweat where I always did: above my upper lip. The sweat 'stache. How exactly was this doctor not passing out from heat exhaustion in those heavy corduroys?

The doctor took a second to look over the sheets I'd filled out. I thought for a moment he might actually just fall asleep right in front of me, but then he looked up again.

"Insomnia, right?'

"That's right. I've always struggled with it. I've found that mari— sorry—the *medicine* has really helped me get a better night's sleep over the years." That was technically true, but it wasn't before I watched four or five episodes of *Seinfeld* and scarfed down a whole container of olives and maybe played a few Steely Dan records and wondered why I didn't play my Steely Dan records more often. After all of that nonsense I would sleep great, sure.

The doctor paused and then looked down at my sheets of paper again.

"What about stomach pain? Do you ever have stomach pain?" he asked.

That was a weirdly specific question.

I thought about it for a few seconds, then answered somewhat sheepishly, "Uh, yeah, as a matter of fact, I've always had a bad stomach." This was *very* true. Why didn't I put *that* down as my reason for needing *medicine*?

He looked back down at the papers.

"What about back pain? Ever have any back pain?" he inquired.

"You know what? I do. I do suffer from occasional back pain. I guess it's a product of being tall. I've always had a stiff back." I don't know why I was extrapolating at this point as the doctor was already ignoring me and jotting down notes.

What was going on here? It was almost as if this doctor wasn't a *doctor* at all but my lawyer who was building a case to defend my reasoning for needing medical marijuana. It was as if this doctor's office was not *entirely* on the up and up. At that moment, all I wanted was to get out of there so I could take a long cold shower and wash away the smell of freshman dorm that had started to permeate my clothes.

"Okay, stand up," he said. "I need to examine you."

Oh, no. I had hoped it wouldn't come to this. Was the doctor turning on me? Was he about to argue for the prosecution and come up with reasons why I shouldn't be given a medical marijuana card? Or was I about to get a greased-up wrinkly old finger in my ass? This day was certainly turning out to be interesting, that's for sure.

I stood up, and out of the desk drawer the doctor retrieved . . . a *stethoscope*. A real live medical instrument. I suddenly felt at ease. This guy was legit! The doctor instructed me to stand by the side of the desk and he pressed the stethoscope against my chest through my T-shirt. I could hardly blame him. I wasn't exactly wild about the idea of exchanging bodily fluids with the skateboarding couple who had been called into the office just before me. After checking my heartbeat, the doctor asked me to breathe in and out while still holding the stethoscope to the centre of my chest. Then he turned around and sat down.

I was expecting an examination a bit more thorough than the kind Dan O'Toole's three-year-old daughter might perform on me with her playtime doctor's kit, but I was also thankful that I would clearly not be getting a wrinkled finger up my ass. He looked down again at the papers and started writing. Finally, after another minute of silent confusion, he spoke.

"I approve you for the use of medical marijuana," he said. And that was that.

He told me to return to the waiting room where I expected to have another chat with ol' dour puss at the front desk. I suspected I would probably have to hand her some hidden fee of twenty or thirty bucks—grease the palms if you will. But as soon as I walked up to her she told me to "sit down" because someone named Tania had just stepped out and would be right back to see me. Who the hell was Tania? What was going on here? I had filled out the entirely unofficial and institutionally suspect medical forms. I had been examined by a doctor who had probably been sued for malpractice back in the '70s and had very likely just returned from some Mexican exile where he performed discount appendix operations until his eyes gave out. Now, I had to wait for some woman named Tania?

The wait was longer than my patience was able to tolerate. The skateboarding couple and the mom from Colorado were long gone. I suspected the mom just gave up and left, while the skateboarding couple were probably at the dispensary choosing between Cheeba

Chews THC gummies and cookies laced with sativa. Meanwhile, a real douchebag-type wearing baggy cargo shorts and a muscle shirt, about fifteen pounds overweight, sat next to me and began talking on his phone, loudly telling the guy at the other end that "he had just landed and he was getting his card so they would be set for Saturday." *Subtle, dude, real subtle.* Maybe think about the people like me who need this medicine to fall asleep, settle my stomach, and fix my back before you shoot your mouth off about your bong party, okay?

When I was just about at my wit's end, Tania finally sauntered in.

Her sartorial sense could be best described as "Eastern European gypsy" mixed with a dash of Mrs. Roper from *Three's Company*. She was probably in her late forties or early fifties with long blond hair. She made a quick stop at the front desk to tell dour girl about the lunch she had just consumed down the beach and then after some back and forth turned around to me and said, "Jay?"

"Yep," I replied.

"Come with me." And with that she walked into the other office next to the waiting room. Perhaps now I was going to get that finger in my ass I had been daydreaming about.

I entered Tania's office and was not at all surprised to find a similar desk and two chairs like those in the doctor's office. But there was another piece of furniture there that did surprise me, if only for a second. At that point, I came to the very quick and correct conclusion that I was about to be ripped off.

"Why do you have an ATM machine in here?" I asked, already knowing the answer.

"Well, you know," she started—her accent was *thick*. Maybe she really was a gypsy. She was most definitely Eastern European. "Many of our customers don't want to use their credit cards. Do you know what I am saying? I want to make it convenient for them to pay for their cards, so it's simple. I have machine put in here and it's simple." *Simple.* It was really very difficult to argue with that logic.

"So you have different choices," said Tania, as she showed me a laminated sheet of paper with several different options. I could buy a licence for six months for $200, nine months for $250, or get an entire year of access to the green stuff for the tidy sum of $300.

This was the moment when most patrons would likely have shown themselves out. There was very little question I was getting ripped off here, but there was another question at hand that often presents itself in situations like this: Do I really feel like going somewhere and doing this all over again? On this particular day, the extra expense was worth it to me, and I didn't even have to use that dirty ATM machine that was staring back at me as I pondered my decision. I had just signed a big new contract with Fox, and this was one of those times when I was going to make a very foolish financial decision for convenience's sake. Because, hey, maybe I wanted to use this licence at some point in the next year, and because I happened to have $300 cash on me at that very moment.

"I'll take the $300 year-long licence, please." For Tania, hearing that sentence was probably better than sex.

"Wonderful," she said with a smile. I was happy to make her day. Tania then turned back to her desk to fill out the official documents. The first would be best described as a certificate, the kind of certificate a five-year-old might get for graduating kindergarten. It consisted of one thick sheet of paper with an official-looking handwritten font that declared me eligible to receive medicine thanks to the thorough medical examination given to me by this very shady doctor. The sheet of paper even featured an embossed gold star in the top corner to make it look properly official. I wondered aloud how many potheads had it framed above their beds.

Tania then went to work on putting together my official California medical marijuana card. She appeared to be deep in concentration. After a minute or so, she turned around and handed me my card. It was the size of a regular business card, but it had two sides and folded like a menu. It was also made of cheap, cheap Bristol board, the kind used to make posters for high school dances and student council election campaigns. It was so cheap I thought it might fall apart in my fingertips. On the front of the card she had simply written, in ball point pen, my name and the date the card expired. On the back there was the same embossed gold star and the doctor's website. She then stood up and took the card from me.

"I'm just going to get the doctor's signature on the card. I will be right back, honey," she said with a smile, as if she had just made all my dreams come true with the cheapest looking piece of "official" medical stationery since the instructions to the *Operation!* board game.

Two minutes later she returned with the card now adorned with the doctor's signature. I left the office like I was leaving a strip club. I felt like I needed a shower to wash off the stench of being ripped off so terribly. Still, I had to admit that I got what I came for. I had managed to secure a medical marijuana card in the great state of California with only a driver's licence, $300, and a bit of charm. Jon Shook and Vinny Dotolo had been right.

The next day, I showed up at the Fox studios proud of myself for actually accomplishing my mission without the assistance of my handler, Susan, or my wife, Chobi. As I recounted my adventure to the *Fox Sports Live* crew, I reached into my wallet to show off my fancy new medical marijuana card, but it was nowhere to be found.

I'd lost it.

Somewhere between that shady doctor's office on the Venice Beach strip and my beachfront condo in Santa Monica, I must have tried to pay for a pupusa from a food truck, and my beautiful, almost completely legit medical marijuana card had fallen to the ground. The whole adventure had been for nothing—not to mention the $300 I'd paid to Gypsy Tania. What a waste!

As the crew laughed at my bad luck and complete incompetence, I couldn't help but wonder if some poor insomniac, who also suffered from stomach and back pain, had found my card on the sidewalk and was right this minute walking into a medical marijuana dispensary to buy some much needed "medicine" using the name Jay Onrait. Hopefully he'd appreciate all the time, money, and hard work I'd put into getting that card but he was likely too stoned to care.

Chapter 11

The Anchorboy Press Tour, Part 1: Getting Bumped for Rob Ford

If you purchased this book it's safe to say you probably read *Anchorboy*. Finishing that book was the culmination of a life-long dream for me. I'd always considered myself a writer first and a broadcaster second, and I had always wanted to be a published writer and have my work available in bookstores. If I never had the chance to publish another book I knew I could live with myself for having accomplished the task at least once.

As exciting as the idea of finishing a book was to me, one of the other things I used to dream about extensively was embarking on an elaborate and lavish press tour to promote said book. Being that I was in the corps of the Canadian media, and that in *Anchorboy* I wrote about the shortcomings and overall lack of dollars available to Canadian media and how it led to other short-comings and downfalls in my career, you would have thought I might have been prepared for what was to come. Having said that, I had never published a book before and had no idea how the process worked in this day and age.

Like most people who love to read, I love to browse the local bookstores (those bookstores that are still open, anyway) any time I get the opportunity. And like most people I have wandered around a bookstore when an author has made an in-store appearance to promote his or her new book, perhaps to read a chapter or two and sign autographs for fans of their work. And like most people I have witnessed such authors sitting there, lonely, sad, and desperate, like a twelve-year-old girl at a junior high school prom waiting for someone to ask her to dance. There may be nothing more devastating in this world than seeing someone so proud of the art they've created sit there and come to the startling realization that absolutely no one else gives a shit.

My friend and *NHL on TSN* host James Duthie embarked on a small version of a press tour for his 2011 book *The Day I (Almost) Killed Two Gretzkys* (a book we would often promote on our old show using the improved and modified title *The Day I Tried to Murder Wayne Gretzky*, under the guise that sensationalism always sells). James regaled me with tales of a dozen or so people showing up at the downtown Chapters in Vancouver. Twitter had just started to sink its claws into the collective consciousness of the sports media world, so getting the word out on his heavily followed Twitter account was really the only way *to* get the word out. The truth is there are very few Jonathan Franzens and Michael Chabons out there who can draw big crowds to bookstores to hear them read their books and answer a few questions. Still, walking past the Barnes and Noble on the 3rd Street Promenade in Santa

Monica just a few blocks from where I now live, I still see a long roster of authors coming to speak and ply their trade for the reading public. The book tour still exists, but like all of book publishing it has been modified to adapt to the times we live in. So, for *Anchorboy*, instead of my dreamed-of two-week trek across the country, I did a two-day media blitz in Toronto, participating in a series of interviews on local and national shows, all culminating in a couple of bookstore appearances and signings.

My first stop on Day One was *Canada AM* with my former *Olympic Morning* partner Beverly Thomson at the CTV studios at 9 Channel Nine Court in Scarborough, the same studios where Dan and I hosted *SportsCentre* for ten years. It felt somewhat like showing up at your ex-girlfriend's house, a little uncomfortable and weird but at the same time familiar. The interview with Bev could not have gone any better, and she even allowed her son to take the morning off school just so he could come in and meet me.

In a way it is always bittersweet when I run into Bev now. I wonder what might have happened had we been paired together on a show long-term. The chemistry between us is always there right away, but more than that it's the fact that Beverly is such a true professional, so kind and warm, the exact type of person you would want hosting your morning show.

After a few goodbye hugs it was a quick stroll down the hall for an interview on CTV News Channel with Jacqueline Milczarek. I remember seeing Jacquie hosting the late-night news on Global Toronto in the late '90s and early aughts and thinking she was a stone-cold fox. I got the distinct impression that Jacquie had not read my book and barely had any help with potential questions. In fact, judging by the questions Jacquie asked me, I came to the quick realization that she had pulled an old trick I used back at *The Big Breakfast* during my A-Channel Manitoba days. She read the book description on the cover and made up the questions from there. Clever girl, that Jacquie. And besides, what author could ever expect an interviewer to read their entire book before an interview? Sure, it would have been nice, but I certainly didn't do it when I was interviewing authors.

While hosting *The Big Breakfast* in Winnipeg back in 1999, I was scheduled to do an interview with Booker prize–winning Australian author Peter Carey of *Oscar and Lucinda* fame. Carey had just completed and was promoting his new novel, a work of historical fiction called *True History of the Kelly Gang*. I was a twenty-five-year-old morning host who was given the book two days in advance. The chances of me tearing through that tome in forty-eight hours were somewhere between slim and none. So I pulled some questions from the jacket copy, and since Carey's a pretty affable guy and a veteran of a million interviews, the eight-minute segment ended up being pretty fun and more than adequate.

The exact opposite would likely have occurred had Margaret Atwood showed up to promote her newly published novel, *The Blind Assassin*, on our show. Atwood was on a major book tour across Canada at the time, and we had managed to secure her for four minutes on our little morning show, leading our main entertainment news host, David J. Roberts, to regale me with horror stories of himself and others who had been charged with interviewing the venerable Canadian titan of arts and letters in the past. The underlying message of interviewing Ms. Atwood: She did not suffer fools gladly and you'd best be prepared. So, just as I had read the entirety of *Moby Dick* in forty-eight bleary-eyed, coffee-fuelled hours leading up to a written exam in first-year English at the University of Alberta, I dove headfirst into her book, took notes, and wrote down the most intelligent set of questions I could muster. With sweat beading on my upper lip the morning Atwood was set to arrive, we received a call at the last minute saying she had run late at a previous interview and with sincere apologies could not make it to our show. I don't know if I have ever felt more relieved to have something *not* work out in my life.

Following the interview with Jacquie I made my way downtown to 299 Queen Street West, the MuchMusic building. En route, my HarperCollins publicist was dispatched to the Burger's Priest a few blocks down Queen Street, just past Spadina Avenue, to grab us both a quick bite of lunch. The Burger's Priest has without a doubt the finest burgers in the city of Toronto and even a secret menu ordering system akin to the famous secret menu at the American In-N-Out Burger chain. I requested a "High Priest," their take on a Big Mac complete with special sauce, and made my way over to the CP24 newsroom where I would be interviewed by Stephen LeDrew.

I had been interviewed by Stephen once before, while promoting the Kraft Celebration Tour with Dan, and found him to be just a delight. I love men who have their own sartorial style, and Stephen has it in droves: shaved pate, well-cut suits, and most importantly a requisite bow tie and signature red eyeglasses. He is well versed in Ontario provincial politics and Toronto city politics and has been kicking around CityTV for a few years as a commentator and host of their noon show. I figured this would be one of the easier interviews of the day, and my good relationship with everyone at CP24 meant I might be able to try something different and fun.

I was to be given a three-minute segment right around 12:15, just when my publicist got back with my burger from Burger's Priest. Therefore, I thought it might be fun if I brought the burger out on set with me for the interview and scarfed it down right in front of Stephen while he asked me questions. Now that I think about it, the whole thing kind of sounds disgusting, but it sure seemed funny when Jay Leno used to bring gyros onto the set of *Late Night with David Letterman* and eat them while Dave asked Jay about life on the road as a comic. At the very least, it might make people stop and take a closer look, which was important on the CP24 News Channel because the screen is always jammed full of clutter—an ongoing traffic and news scroll, a five-day weather forecast, an ad or two jammed in there, and finally up in the top corner a small window with the actual newscast.

I waited patiently in the CP24 green room, where former Canadian Olympic bike racer and Pert shampoo commercial star Curt Harnett was waiting to be on the show to promote a charity event that weekend. Curt is famous both for being an Olympian and for possessing Olympic-worthy locks of curly blond hair that he often holds back from his head with a pair of Oakley sunglasses. I found him to be a genuinely nice guy and was having a delightful conversation with the man when I was suddenly summoned from the green room by a producer with a headset and informed that I would be on in three minutes.

Stephen greeted me warmly and cracked a few jokes about whether or not I had actually written the book myself. He had a warm and friendly nature about him and was pretty amused by my little burger prank. I offered Stephen some fries and asked him how his family was doing, but he was more interested in hearing about Los Angeles and life at Fox. We made some small talk and before I knew it the three-minute commercial break was up. "Here we go!" said Stephen.

STEPHEN: Jay Onrait is here to discuss his new book, *Anchorboy*, and to eat his lunch as well . . .

JAY: Have you ever been to the Burger's Priest down the street, Stephen?

STEPHEN: Yeah, what is that you have there?

JAY: Why don't you try one of these fries? This is a High Priest. Have you heard of their secret menu, Ste—

STEPHEN (interrupting): Jay, I'm going to have to cut you off there. It appears Toronto mayor Rob Ford is speaking to the media. Let's go live to Queen's Park . . .

I was a little startled.

By now you probably know the incredibly bizarre tale of Toronto's overindulgent mayor and part-time crack aficionado, Rob Ford. To put the timeline in perspective: *Toronto Star* reporter Robyn Doolittle and the website Gawker had claimed to have seen Ford in a crudely shot video that took place at the house of a drug dealer near the city's Jane and Finch area. In it, they claimed the mayor smoked crack cocaine out of a pipe with at least two other men who were known criminals, one of whom had been killed just three months previously. To that point, no actual footage of the video had been made public, just a still shot of Ford standing with the two men. Doolittle and other reporters who claimed to have seen it staked their reputations on the fact that it was indeed Ford in the video. Up until that point, the embattled mayor had denied all allegations. That particular day, however, something changed in the mayor's strategy for dealing with the scandal. Either he or someone in his camp had clearly seen the tape and determined the footage was real, or his lawyer had decided that a more open strategy needed to be taken. That morning, Rob Ford was about to shock the shit out of the city of Toronto and most of North America.

CP24 cut away from me and Stephen directly to a swarm of reporters surrounding Mayor Ford just outside Toronto's City Hall. The questions had already begun, but there was a strange tone to the proceedings. I tried to listen as I stuffed french fry after french fry into my big mouth. The entire newsroom was practically silent—a very unusual situation.

"What was that question you asked me back in May?" said Ford to no reporter in particular. The reporter and his fellow press corps thought for a second to try to determine exactly what the mayor was getting at.

"What did you ask me back in May? You can ask me again," repeated Ford.

Finally one of the reporters went for it: "Have you ever smoked crack cocaine?"

"There you go," said Ford, and then paused. "Yes, I have smoked crack cocaine."

Well, there goes my interview, I thought to myself.

I have never in my life heard an entire working television news-room make a collective audible gasp like they did when Ford uttered those six words. Imagine everything that these people had been privy to in their lifetimes covering the news on a daily basis: murder, rape, various types of injustice both at home and abroad. Someone who has to cover this kind of horrifying behaviour and its consequences every single day will eventually start to become numb. Sending an entire television newsroom into a state of shock would take a truly significant event. This was that significant event.

Everyone looked at each other with mouths agape. About two full seconds went by before the news director took charge of the situation and began to bark out orders to her assignment editors and writers. To a veteran news director this was like winning the lottery. Before this, most people just speculated that the Rob Ford crack tape existed but they would likely never see it. News and gossip website Gawker had raised enough money to purchase the tape through a Kickstarter fund, but they had lost contact with the reported owner of the video and donated the funds to charity instead. But clearly, someone in the Ford camp had seen the tape or at least decided it was a real thing, and now they had chosen to get ahead of the story by issuing a public *mea culpa*. The mayor of Toronto, fourth largest city in North America, was telling a group of gathered reporters that he had smoked crack cocaine.

I dropped the french fry that had been situated between my thumb and forefinger when I heard the news. I looked at Stephen as he turned to me.

"I think your interview is over," he said.

"I know."

Stephen tried to apologize but I was having none of it. I had been in the business long enough to know when a writer was going to get bumped, and getting bumped because the mayor of Canada's largest city admitted to smoking crack on live television was a pretty respectable way to get bumped.

My only concern was the remainder of the day. I still had several television and radio interviews left to go. Would anyone have time for me now that their resources were going to be dedicated to covering this new Ford revelation? Furthermore, what about the reading public? Would any of them even remember any of the interviews if all their attention had been justifiably taken away by this breakthrough? Was there a chance that all the hard work I had done to promote the book could be completely wiped away by the confessions of an overweight and drug-addicted sensualist who was guiding civic politics in the Greater Toronto Area? I tried not to let it depress me as I sheepishly wandered back toward the green room, with the audio technician who had put a microphone on me chasing after me to get his mic back. I made some more small talk with Curt Harnett, who had also been bumped from his segment, and then collected my things and left. *Rob Ford*, I thought to myself, *what a fucking asshole.*

Chapter 12

The Anchorboy Press Tour, Part 2: Old Friends

The old MuchMusic studio—a studio that has hosted count-less famous musicians and countless VJs introducing countless poorly shot Canadian videos—is now home to *The Social*, a daytime talk show in the vein of ABC's *The View*. *The Social* is the brainchild of Melissa Grelo. Melissa co-hosted our *Olympic Morning* coverage back in Vancouver 2010 up in Whis-tler, and much like me she received positive reviews and praise, plus a general sense that it might lead to a career boost once she returned home. Unfortunately, also like me, she received no such advancement or promotion after *Olympic Morning*. In the case of Melissa, though, it had nothing to do with her talent and certainly nothing to do with her looks (she's a knockout). Rather, it seemed to have everything to do with the biggest problem facing Canadian television since the industry began—a lack of shows. There was simply nowhere to move Melissa that wouldn't have meant jettisoning a perfectly capable host out of an already occupied spot.

For the two years following the Vancouver Olympics, Melissa and I would meet regularly for coffee and basically lament the lack of progress in our careers. I kept her up to date on my ultimately failed attempt to launch a Canadian version of *The Soup*, and she kept me up to date on her continuing attempts to launch a Canadian version of *The View*. Ultimately, through dogged persistence and a staggering work ethic, Melissa prevailed in her quest, and CTV agreed to put the show on right after *The Marilyn Denis Show* starting in the fall of 2013, just before *Anchorboy* hit the shelves. The catch? Melissa was going to continue as co-host of the CP24 morning show. That meant Mel would be working almost twelve-hour days for the chance to realize her dream of her own Canadian daytime talk show. But it was her own choice; the tenuous nature of Canadian television success made her feel it was necessary. Welcome once again to the glamorous world of Canadian TV!

To promote my book, I was going to join the cast of *The Social* as the fifth co-host. I figured the show would give me the perfect opportunity to reach exactly the right audience for *Anchorboy*: moms, moms, and more moms—the kind of moms who would (hopefully) be searching for that perfect gift to put in their son's or husband's stocking for the Christmas season. All I had to do was be charming and funny.

Melissa was hosting that afternoon alongside another *Olympic Morning* veteran from Vancouver, Elaine "Lainey" Lui. As I walked into the studio, I saw Lainey sitting at a table in the middle of the room checking her phone, every few seconds taking a big pull off an e-cigarette that she kept close by. I sat down next to her, and we began chatting about her move to Vancouver. She was born and raised in Toronto, but like many Torontonians who find themselves in Vancouver for work, school, or whatever, she never had a desire to come back east. Vancouver has that amazing pull for so many people. Lainey had her own business with her megapopular website and really didn't need to be in the so-called centre of the Canadian media universe full time. She expressed no desire to ever return to Toronto, despite the fact that she spoke with her mom daily and her mom lived there. But the lure of being one of the stars on *The Social* was obviously enough to finally convince her and her husband to make the cross-country move. It was hard to tell if she was enjoying herself because it was always hard to tell if she was enjoying herself. But I was happy to see her. I may or may not have had a mild crush.

Seconds later I was called into the circle of hosts. Literally. All the other hosts including a pregnant Melissa gathered around in a circle and joined hands and said a little motivational prayer, something that had never happened to me before in my near twenty-year career in television. It was kind of nice. I decided I would have to try it with Dan sometime—only it would just be the two of us holding hands and staring directly at each other. Might be a tough sell.

Not surprisingly, the topic of discussion that day had taken a recent and rather shocking turn. Whatever the gaggle of super-cute producers had originally planned for the show had been thrown into a large trash bin behind 299 Queen and replaced with Rob Ford, Rob Ford, and more Rob Ford. At least this was a topic I could speak somewhat intelligently about, having just had two years of hard work swept aside by a mayor who had a little problem controlling his appetites. This was actually going to be fun. The studio audience seemed to consist of about seventy-five or so moms and their best girlfriends and one slightly familiar dude sitting in the back row. Where had I seen that guy before?

We got a nice standing ovation from the crowd and we were off. Melissa kept things rolling along with questions and talking points. She was always a great host at CP24 and now she was really in her element. *The Social* is perfectly suited to her strengths, and I was so happy she had achieved her goal of getting her own show on the air. I managed to get a few laughs for my story about Mayor Ford interrupting my interview on CP24 earlier that day. The crowd seemed to respond well to my *Anchorboy* stories, and I think I might have even sold a few books. I knew my own mom was watching at home and was probably pretty happy. In other words, everything was going well.

But who was that lone guy in the back row?

At one point during the discussion about Ford, right before the first commercial break, Melissa asked the audience members if any of them had an opinion about the recent Ford revelation, and a couple of the show's producers (there seemed to be about twenty of them) stood by with handheld microphones, ready to leap into the crowd for instant interaction. The man in the back row was the first to raise his hand and I suddenly realized who he was.

He was there to see me, and this was about to get weird.

Dana McKiel is a man who never ages. He looks the same today as the first time I met him back in 1994. I had known the man in the back row for twenty years, and I probably owed him as much credit for my career as anyone. Dana was a lifer at Rogers Community Cable channels all across Ontario, but mostly in the Toronto area. He had been an on-air host for Rogers Community Cable for longer than anyone in the province. He was a huge part of their Ontario university, college, and high school sports broadcasts, either doing play-by-play or hosting.

Dana was an incredibly friendly and chatty character who dressed a little bit like a used car salesman and probably would have been great at selling just about anything. But he also loved sports. I mean *loved* sports. It takes a pretty special person to continue to follow and maintain a passion for amateur sports for so many years beyond just following the exploits of your own kids. Dana was a man who was truly born to be a host on his channel. He was really perfect, and Rogers was very lucky to have him.

Just a month or so into my first year at Ryerson I saw a posting on the bulletin board in the audio laboratory, where we spliced together reel-to-reel tape and hosted radio shows. The posting asked for a reporter for Rogers Community Cable live sports events throughout the Toronto area. An actual on-air position while you were attending broadcasting school—albeit *not* a paying one. I was almost vibrating, I was so determined to get the job. I knew there were several other people at Ryerson, not just in my class but second- and third-year students as well, who would be just as desperate to get the job as I was. Ultimately, what sealed the job for me were two things: volunteering at ITV News in Edmonton during my second year at the University of Alberta, and more importantly, asking the nice crew at ITV News to allow me five minutes of on-camera reading from the teleprompter. This awkward, stiff, and rather robotic performance formed the basis of my very first demo tape, of which I carried at least five VHS copies around with me at all times. I mailed a copy of the VHS demo to Dana and about a week later got a message on my answering machine in my dorm room on the sixth floor of Pitman Hall.

"Hi, Jay, it's Dana McKiel calling from Rogers Cable 10. We'd like to bring you on board, big guy!"

I went sprinting out of my dorm room and leapt over a couch in the common area of the senior suite I was sharing with four other students, like I was a young Perdita Felicien during Canadian Olympic trials. My friend Allan Thrush, who now works as a freelance editor and producer in Calgary, says it was one of the funniest things he has ever seen in his life, watching me prance around like a gazelle and scream "Yes!" while double-pumping my fists in the air. I was oblivious to how ridiculous I looked at the time. In my mind, then and now, it was this break that truly got my career started. Even my first real on-air paying job at Global Saskatoon didn't carry the same weight that this volunteer reporter job carried. And having to compete with my fellow would-be sports broadcasters who were just as determined to break into the business and get started made it all the sweeter. I will always be grateful to Dana for choosing me to come report for him.

The job involved several different responsibilities. I would put together two- to three-minute reports for Dana's show *Sports Week Magazine*, which featured news about amateur sports around Toronto and Southern Ontario. I would also serve as the sideline reporter on live events that Rogers Cable was broadcasting, like Ontario women's university volleyball games and high school hoops tournaments.

I was generally stiff and awkward, and at one point during a live broadcast of a women's basketball game between York and Guelph universities I completely froze in what was very likely the single most embarrassing on-air moment of my life. I had never done live television before and simply wasn't prepared for it. I tried to memorize what I was going to say, which is *never* a good idea in a live TV situation. At one point when Dana threw over to me on the sideline I said something along the lines of: "Thanks, Dana. The Guelph women's team has been a formidle . . . a formidable squad throughout the first three weeks of women's basketball play . . . I . . . York women's team is three and two coming in . . . I . . . the girls . . . good match . . . back to you." And then I produced a look on my face that was somewhere between disappointment and shame.

Dana handled it beautifully and pretended that Craig Sager himself had just thrown it back to him: "Great stuff, Jay. Thanks very much!" Upon returning home, my very kind college roommates could not hide their embarrassment at what they had just seen on live television, which was then followed by merciless ridicule, all of which made me feel much better.

Over the course of the next twenty years or so, I ran into Dana randomly at various sporting events around Toronto. He was always in a great mood and super chatty, talking about some new project he was embarking on or some new job he was applying for. I just loved his good-natured personality. He was definitely a talker, perhaps sometimes a little too much. Ultimately, though, I've always appreciated that first big break he gave me and so I was always happy to see him.

That day on *The Social*, however, I had mixed feelings when I saw him in the audience.

"Any thoughts from our audience on Rob Ford's recent admission on live television that he did, in fact, smoke crack?"

Dana's hand shot up to the sky and a young producer chased after it.

"I have a few things to say," began Dana.

I gripped the bottom of my chair tighter. *Please don't mention me, please don't mention me.*

"First of all, I'd like to say congratulations to my good friend Jay Onrait on the publication of his book, *Anchorboy*. I think it's terrific and we go back a long way." The other panel members all glanced my way and I jumped in with a quick reply.

"That's right. Dana McKiel, everybody! He gave me my first big break in the business." I looked around nervously, hoping this is where it would end.

But this was live television. And Dana McKiel was on a roll.

Before I could say "crack cocaine," Dana had begun parrying back and forth with the panel, enthusiastically sharing his opinions on the day's big news.

Now, in all fairness to the guy, I know he was in the audience to support me. But Dana is a man who loves to talk, and despite his best intentions, his enthusiasm and television instincts won out that day. What began as a few quick one-liners rapidly developed into a full blown discussion about the man of the hour—Rob Ford.

I sat there slowly curling and twisting the copy of *Anchorboy* that was sitting in front of me, like I was wringing out a washcloth, all the while silently muttering to myself how this was supposed to be about me. Remember my book, guys? *Anchorboy*? I flew all the way from L.A. for this!

Finally, sensing the audience's growing disinterest—and my growing discomfort—Melissa stepped in. "Okay, sir. Well, thanks for your time but we have to take a commercial break. We'll be back with more *Social* after this." It turns out they'd used up all the designated audience feedback time talking to Dana and now we were moving on to another segment. *Good grief.*

Melissa and the other ladies began to chat amongst themselves, while the lead producer of the show approached our table with a disapproving young assistant by her side. I thought she would address the situation with Melissa, perhaps offer some guidance on how to deal with overly enthusiastic audience members who monopolize air time, but instead the producer looked right at me.

"Do you know that guy?" she asked.

Everyone on the panel—Melissa, Lainey, Cynthia, and Traci—turned toward me as I replied, "Yes. I know him." I explained my connection to Dana as quickly as I could. Time was of the essence here.

The producer was visibly irritated. "He showed up and we were going to let another lady into the audience, but we let him in because he said he knew you."

Great. Not only had my previous interview been sabotaged, but now I had unknowingly sabotaged Melissa's show because of my past connections. I looked out to the back row of the audience and Dana gave me an enthusiastic wave. I waved back tentatively. Soon this would all be over. In fact, sooner than I realized. I thought I would be on as co-host for the entire show, but in fact I was actually on for only the first half-hour—a built-in fail-safe in case one of their guests turned out to be an unequivocal disaster, like me. I bid goodbye to Melissa, Lainey, and the many producers, and I was off.

As I was walking out of the studio, Dana called out to me. "I'll see you at your book signing!"

I did my best to avoid eye contact, but I couldn't hold back a smile. This trip could not possibly get any more weird, could it?

The next day, the trip got weirder.

Chapter 13

The Anchorboy Press Tour, Part 3: The Iron Sheik

Throughout my life, I have always had a complicated relationship with the CBC. Growing up, it was a huge part of my household entertainment, and as I detailed in *Anchorboy*, CBC Edmonton and its local sportscasts were a big part of why I decided to become a sportscaster in the first place. When you live the first nine years of your life in a prairie town of only 700 people, and the Internet has yet to be invented, the CBC is your lifeline to the world.

I watched the CBC in the morning as a little kid, starting every day with the familiar recorder-accompanied theme song to *The Friendly Giant*, a show that consisted of a friendly giant who lived alone in a castle with a rooster and a giraffe. It seems like an odd interspecies relationship looking back now, but everyone I knew was keen on the giant's signature phrase: "Look up, waaaay up, and I'll call Rusty." Rusty, in this case, was the rooster that the giant may or may not have been having an inappropriate relationship with at the time. Rusty "lived" in what appeared to be a burlap sack hanging from the wall. I have no idea how he got out of there to poo or have a bite of a sunflower seed or two for sustenance.

The Friendly Giant was followed by *Mr. Dressup* starring Pennsylvania native Ernie Coombs as a guy who basically sat around his house all day singing songs, drawing surprisingly lifelike pictures, and dressing up in costumes that appeared magically inside his Tickle Trunk—a red steel trunk painted with flowers that sat in his living room. He had a puppet dog Finnegan and a puppet son Casey. Parental status was never really clarified, and we never saw any trace of a wife/mother, or any woman in his life for that matter. Parents were not supposed to question the fact that he was a single man who dressed up in costumes all day that were situated in something called a Tickle Trunk. Or that he was named Mr. Dressup. All of this seemed perfectly logical and acceptable in the '70s and '80s.

The CBC primetime lineup was a huge part of my life at the time as well. *Beachcombers* was a half-hour sitcom about, well, beachcombers who competed for logs and such in Gibsons, BC, starring an Italian man named Bruno Gerussi as a Greek man named Nick Adonidas whose arch-rival Relic wore a famous toque and owned the shittiest boat ever seen on television. This was followed every Sunday night by *The Wonderful World of Disney*. I watched every single Escape from Witch Mountain movie and Love Bug film, but I prayed every week that we might be blessed with an actual Mickey and Friends cartoon. No Teletoon or Cartoon Network available for this kid. An episode of *Sport Goofy* was like being given a large bag of gold.

But as I grew older, I started to become aware of how truly terrible a lot of the programming on the network was. The big Monday night anchor during my early teens was *Danger Bay*, which starred Hollywood veteran Donnelly Rhodes as marine biologist "Doc" Roberts, who was raising two kids while presumably solving crimes that involved whale poaching, all the while hitting on his hot helicopter pilot friend who provided the necessary sexual tension needed to keep the show interesting. My former TSN co-anchor Cory Woron was a child actor in the Vancouver area and actually appeared on the show at least once as the best friend of Doc Roberts' son Jonah, a feather-haired tennis-playing little douchebag. For years in my thirties, after Cory had relayed this information, I begged friends who worked at the CBC to find the lost Cory Woron footage, but alas, as of now it has still gone unseen by these eyes. More interesting to any heterosexual male my age in the country at the time was Doc Roberts' daughter, played by Hellman's mayonnaise heir Ocean Hellman. American teenage boys may have had Alyssa Milano, but we had an Ocean.

As I got older and my cable packages got better, I saw less and less of the CBC, even from a news standpoint. Only the venerable *Hockey Night in Canada*, the Olympics, and CFL broadcasts kept me coming back to the public broadcaster. I didn't think about the fact that the CBC was taking a portion of my taxes until I actually entered the television business as an on-air broadcaster in 1999 in Saskatoon. Soon after I arrived in the spectacular Saskatchewan city, I was introduced to Piya Chattopadhyay through my friend and news co-anchor Chris Krieger.

Piya was a born-and-raised Saskatoon girl who went to high school at Marion Graham and attended the University of Saskatchewan. Like me she moved on from there to Ryerson in Toronto and had returned to the province to take her first television job as a reporter with the CBC. Piya and I did not like each other at first for reasons that are still somewhat unclear to me—I was a douchebag? She was a douchebag? Who knows. But we became the best of friends during my year working in the city, and she was kind enough to include me in her circle of Saskatoon pals on regular nights out drinking pint after pint of Sangria downtown at the Black Duck pub (I realize we were not supposed to be drinking Sangria out of pint glasses but we were twenty-four years old at the time).

I also managed to cause Piya some significant stress during my short time living in her city. I was the last person out of her door following a pre-drinking session at her apartment one evening, and I called out to her as she walked down the street, "Do you want me to lock this?"

"Don't worry about it," she replied.

We'd all had a few drinks but I was certainly sober enough to make a judgment call. Should I just lock it anyway? *Nah*, I thought to myself. *What's the worst that could happen?*

Hours later, several of us returned to her place for a post-drinking session and found the entire apartment empty. Ransacked. They had taken *everything* she owned. It was as if someone had been watching us leave and immediately backed a truck up to the front door and started hauling everything out casually like movers. Amazingly, she had home insurance at her young age, so she received a nice settlement. Thankfully, I only leave the door unlocked of apartments occupied by responsibly insured adults. She never let me forget the fact that I was last to leave, and it was probably all my fault that she had lost her copy of *OK Computer* on CD.

Piya seemed rich to the rest of us working in the television news industry in Saskatoon at the time, and that's because she was a CBC employee in a federal union. Reporter salaries at the

CBC were standardized across the country. She was making almost twice what those of us at CTV and Global were making. Years later, I realized that working at the CBC was a little like playing in the CFL. If the salaries were going to be the same all across the country, then it was better to play for Winnipeg or Saskatchewan than Toronto or BC, because your dollar would stretch a lot further.

On the second day of my "book tour," I did a handful of newspaper, radio, and television interviews around town, then spent the afternoon in the hallowed halls of the Canadian Broadcast Company. My first stop was at the radio show *Q*, a popular interview program then hosted by former Moxy Früvous lead singer and noted teddy bear aficionado Jian Ghomeshi. Jian was out that day, and I was thrilled to learn that Piya would be filling in. How strange and wonderful was this experience? Two friends who had known each other since they first got into the media business now involved in a one-on-one interview about a book one of those friends had written about the media business. The interview went really well. Piya was even a little nervous because it was her first time filling in on the show. The studio was set up with Persian rugs on the floor where bands would often play acoustic sets on the program. I participated in a Vine video where I rolled myself up in one of them, but the joke turned out to be on me as the carpets had clearly not been cleaned since the show went on the air and were filled with the dirt and mud of a thousand stinky indie-rock boots.

I left the interview feeling so much better. So what if my media tour wasn't going exactly as planned, so what if my interview on CP24 had been interrupted by an out-of-control crackhead politician, and so what if my interview on *The Social* had been interrupted by a good friend and former employer who didn't know when to stop talking? The important thing was that I was getting the word out about *Anchorboy*. Q was extremely popular, and I was fortunate Piya and her producers were willing to have me on to talk. Immediately, my Twitter feed fired up with tons of positive feedback about the segment with Piya. My agent, Carly Watters, and editor, Doug Richmond, along with my publicist, had come to the taping at the CBC, and now the four of us got into an elevator and headed to the final stop of the day: *George Stroumboulopoulos Tonight*.

You may have noticed that on the back of *Anchorboy* there's a quote from George Stroumboulopoulos that reads: "I can't remember if we've ever met or if I've even heard Jay Onrait speak, but I do know that a book from him at this stage must mean he's set to retire . . . so it can't be all bad, right?" I *wish* I was all set to retire! I love that quote—and it's more accurate than most people probably realize. George and I barely know each other at all. I met him at a Gemini Awards ceremony a couple years ago, and that was pretty much it. He probably wasn't lying when he said he couldn't remember!

So why did I reach out to him for a quote on the back of my book? Because my publisher, HarperCollins, asked me to, I thought it was a decent idea, and George was more than happy to oblige. Admittedly, I also had a somewhat ulterior motive. If a quote from George made its way onto the back of my book, then surely George would invite me to appear for an interview on his television show. George has a fascinating interview style that involves sitting directly across from his subject and leaning forward so that his face is just inches away. Then, he gazes into the subject's eyes with an intensity that suggests he is staring into their very soul. I was looking forward to sitting in the red club chair across from George and making every effort not to laugh as he stared deep into my eyes and asked me:

"Jay, is it true you have a serious problem controlling your bowels?"

That opportunity never came. When I was sent the list of interviews I would be doing for *Anchorboy* in Toronto, *George Stroumboulopoulos Tonight* was on the list, but I wasn't going to be interviewed one-on-one: I would be part of a panel. This meant sitting around a table with George and two comedians, riffing on some of the subjects of the day—a time filler that allowed the show not to have to find a worthy interview subject for every segment. I figured there must be a pretty exciting guest booked on the show that day.

When I got off the elevator where George's studio was located, I was suddenly face-to-face with Steven and Chris. Steven Sabados and Chris Hyndman were the new faces of afternoon television on the CBC—the former stars of *Designer Guys* on HGTV Canada now had a daily lifestyle show on the public broadcaster, and they had just finished taping for the day. I lived in a beautiful condo building at the corner of Queen Street East and Sumach Street in the east end of downtown Toronto from 2003 to 2006, and I would often pass the two of them in a Lexus SUV as I entered and left the parking garage. Their office must be in this building, I always thought to myself. (I am not exactly a genius when it comes to perception.) They came out as a couple a few years later. I snapped a quick photo with Chris because he looks like Dan O'Toole if Dan dyed his hair, and to me that is hilarious.

I was led to the green room by Carly Heffernan, a former member of Toronto's Sketchersons comedy troupe, whom I had met years earlier while hosting the troupe's *Sunday Night Live* show. Carly has the manic energy of a sketch comedian and is always "on." We cracked jokes all the way to the small room where everyone gathered on couches to munch on what was without question the worst food in the history of television talk show green rooms. George had recently gone vegan, and (I mean this with the utmost love and respect possible) he looked absolutely terrible. He looked like Adrien Brody preparing for his Oscar-winning role in *The Pianist*. I was genuinely concerned for the guy. In keeping with George's new lifestyle, the spread in the green room mostly consisted of dried apple chips that were so tasteless I think I would have rather had George spoon feed sand into my mouth. I grabbed a bag to take on the set and hopefully have a little fun. Then the producer of the panel segment, Steven Kerzner, walked into the room.

Fans of Canadian comedy and pop culture may recognize that name. For years Steven plied his trade at various media outlets as the alter ego of the curmudgeonly, cigar-chomping puppet Ed the Sock. Ed was a mainstay on MuchMusic during the 1990s and was especially well known for his "worst of" end-of-the-year video show, *Fromage*, which for several years was one of the funniest, most-underrated things on Canadian television. He also hosted his own talk show that appeared Friday nights on CityTV. Ed was paired with various co-hosts over the life of his talk show, culminating in Kerzner's real-life wife serving as co-host for the final years of the program. In a weird coincidence, his brothers Mitch and Jordan were both longtime employees of TSN as a producer and editor, respectively. I had known Jordan, the youngest Kerzner brother, since my first days at TSN in 1996. I had never met Steven, however, and I had no idea that he was now producing these comedy segments on George's show. Steven was a short, slight, and talkative guy and we hit it off right away, going back and forth and riffing on the recent news about Mayor Ford. Steven told me he was also writing a book under his Ed the Sock persona and that he had read mine and enjoyed it. I immediately felt a rapport with the guy and began to look forward to the panel segment more and more.

Joining me on the panel were two local comedians. Arthur Simeon was just starting out in the business as a stand-up, and Emma Hunter was mostly focused on sketch work but was now also branching into stand-up, having recently appeared on a City/Much game show about pop culture. Cute and bubbly, she seemed destined to play the romantic love interest on a future CBC work-place sitcom. Both Arthur and Emma were friendly and laid-back, but I noticed something distinctly different about the way they pre-pared for the segment. They *prepared* for the segment. Steven had been in contact with both of them about the proposed discussion points, including the recent breaking news about Mayor McCrack-head. Both comedians were armed with a page full of potential one-liners and jokes to say during the discussion.

I had nothing but my bag of apple chips.

I hoped I wasn't going to make a fool of myself out there, unless it was on purpose like I usually did when I appeared on shows like this.

The "exciting guest" on the show that day was former Cana-dian prime minister Joe Clark. I guess if you have to be bumped, then getting bumped by a former head of state is nothing to be ashamed of. (You've probably noticed that I am great at justify-ing reasons for being bumped from interviews at this point in my career.) I had basically been following Joe around town for two days from interview to interview. It began the previous morning when we met in the green room at *Canada AM*, and then I fol-lowed him over to CTV News Channel, at which point he was clearly becoming uncomfortable trying to make small talk with me since he had absolutely no idea who I was. I tried the "we're both from Alberta" angle, but that can only take you so far. Joe was nice though and a consummate politician, asking me about my book and what life was like in Los Angeles. I'd lost touch with the former PM after my appearance on *The Social*, but now was back in contact with him as I watched George stare straight into his thick glasses and jowly jaws from the green room monitor at the CBC. George had Mr. Clark on for *two* full segments to discuss his new book, and although I could only hear bits and pieces of it in between Steven, Arthur, and Emma talking about their plans for our upcoming segment, I have no doubt that the former prime minister would have been a fascinating interview.

A few minutes later, another staffer appeared in the green room doorway to let us know that the PM's interview was finished and we were on next. We were led to the main studio past another gaggle of employees, many of whom were just standing around idly and chatting. All of my darkest thoughts about the CBC suddenly came bubbling up to the surface of my brain. Why were my taxpayer dollars funding this bloated talk show that seemed to lack direction and—if the recent Nielsen ratings were to be believed—viewers? I decided then and there that it was time for me to stir up some shit . . .

I took my seat around an elevated table in the middle of a large studio. The audience surrounding us were sitting "in the round" like it was a stop on Def Leppard's *Hysteria* tour in 1989. George and I greeted each other warmly—he had clearly not read the book, but again, I couldn't really blame the guy. He had just finished interviewing Joe Clark for eight minutes; I would have spent the previous evening cramming for that too. Arthur and Emma had appeared on the show before and so we were off and running as soon as the red light went on.

George opened the segment by stating how nice it was to have Helen Fielding on that day, the author of *Bridget Jones's Diary*, "that book that you read that makes you say 'Oh my God if my life is like this

I have to change it.'" I had never read *Bridget Jones's Diary* but I wondered how many people had read *my* book and thought the same thing. Also, Helen Fielding was on? I didn't see her anywhere. Clearly our segment would be paired with an interview George had done a different day. This whole production was certainly strange.

"I have to take bigger risks," George continued. "I need to explore the concept of risks because we all need a little nudging in that direction." Was George talking about me? Or was he talking about himself? George had just completed a ten-episode run of a new interview show for CNN. George's show was put in a pretty tough ratings position right from the start. CNN had placed it on Sunday nights when people in their 30s, 40s, and 50s who might want to watch it were probably preoccupied with *Mad Men*, *Game of Thrones*, and the other premium cable gems of the day. His U.S. television run had already ended by the time I visited his CBC show that day, and as he made no mention of it, I didn't think it was appropriate to bring it up. I knew firsthand how hard it was to launch something new on U.S. television, especially in this day and age, and I felt genuinely gutted that the CNN show hadn't worked out for George—especially since I knew he kept a place in Los Angeles and really wanted to make the leap.

George introduced me warmly, welcomed me back from the States, and mentioned my book, ticking all the boxes, while asking how I was. I had been given a peel-off sticker that said "Visitor #3-7452" to place on my suit jacket while walking through the CBC and I mentioned that I was "happy my taxpayer dollars had allowed me the privilege to wear such a sticker." The joke fell flatter than George's ratings at CNN. Why was everyone at the CBC so afraid to talk about the millions of dollars we Canadians were spending to fund this national network? I guess I just answered my own question.

George turned over to Emma and asked her about the last time she took a big risk. I guess this was the theme of our segment today, and there was no doubt I had a good angle to bring to the discussion. Emma launched into a joke about how during the past Thanksgiving she decided to "attack her uncle from Alaska across the Bering Strait to Asia, and held North America. That's why they call it Risk!" That joke fell flatter than my taxpayer joke. The afternoon crowd at the CBC had clearly spent too much time exploring the Hockey Hall of Fame earlier in the day, or maybe we were all just terrible—either way this was bad TV. As it turns out, we were just getting started with the whole "bad TV" thing.

"What's one risk you would never take?" George asked me after we had all bantered back and forth for a few minutes.

I looked down at the flimsy, cheap plastic red water cups on the table.

"I'll tell you one risk I would never take: using thermos tops as mugs on the George Stroumboulopoulos show." *Zing!*

"I don't want to make you feel badly about your choices, dude," said George as he moved in closer to my face. Why did he insist on doing that? "but the World Food Program 'Fill the Cup' campaign, that's what these mugs are for."

"But that's just what you did, you made me feel bad!" I replied. "You did the exact opposite of what you said you were going to do! You said 'I don't want to make you feel bad,' and then you made me feel bad about it!'" This was met with actual laughter and applause from the audience, which meant we had something resembling a fun exchange going on. At that point, George had to go to commercial break, just as we were gaining a little momentum. Still, the whole panel segment wasn't actually that bad. So I didn't get my one-on-one close-proximity face-to-face time on a nationally broadcasted Canadian talk show that drew the same number of viewers as reruns of poker on TSN—it didn't matter. I showed up ready to play and I was holding my own with these comedians. This really wasn't a waste of time after all.

During the commercial break, the floor director told me everything was going well. I was feeling very happy about the entire proceedings, but against all odds, this bizarre and bewildering couple of days spent promoting my little book was about to get even weirder.

After we returned from the break George addressed me once again. I was feeling a little bad about George asking me all the questions during the roundtable and leaving Emma and Arthur out in the cold.

"Justin Trudeau recently admitted he smokes weed. A lot of people said, 'That's so progressive,' but then others said, 'Hey, I think that's illegal.' Do you think that was a reasonable risk?"

Why was George coming to me with this one and not the two comedians? I wondered? Didn't it stand to reason that comedians would be better versed on marijuana than a sportscaster? Then again, maybe not.

"Actually, I do," I said. "Politically, it separates him from the other candidates, and it makes his views stand out. And it's not crack." Good ol' Rob Ford had provided me the ammunition I needed to make a timely joke.

George continued: "Speaking of taking risks, I know you loved old-school wrestling. Did you ever want to take a risk and become a pro wrestler?"

Where the hell was this going?

"Yes, George," I replied, "just look at my physique. Clearly."

"What I used to love about wrestling was how controversial and risk taking it was in terms of politics. Talking to different parts of the world, introducing us to Middle Eastern cultures . . ."

"Yeah, that's right!" I chimed in. "The Iron Sheik and Nikolai Volkoff."

"You did love the Iron Sheik, right?" asked George.

"Big-time fan of the Iron Sheik," I replied.

Where was this going? What the hell was wrong with George? Fidgeting in his seat, eyes darting around the room. Suddenly I turned around—and there he was.

"Oh, my gosh," I said like some yokel.

The Iron Sheik himself, draped in Iranian desert robes and keffiyeh, with a big gold medallion around his neck. He walked up to our table trailed by a heavyset younger dude wearing a green and red plaid jacket and sideways ball cap with some sort of makeshift championship wrestling belt over his shoulder. All I could think to do was stare into the camera. *Straight into the camera.* It all made sense to me now, about as much sense as an appearance by the Iron Sheik on a Canadian talk show in 2013 could make.

The Iron Sheik was a legendary old grappler who rode the wave of pro-wrestling popularity in the World Wrestling Federation throughout the '80s and early 1990s as a villainous "heel" who terrorized good guys like Hulk Hogan and Sgt. Slaughter (Hogan won his first ever WWF title from the Sheik in 1984). The Sheik memorably teamed up with Russian tough guy Nikolai Volkoff to form one of the most memorable tag teams in wrestling history. They would get booed mercilessly by crowds when they entered the ring, as Volkoff insisted on singing the Russian national anthem before matches while the Sheik stood by holding an Iranian flag. The Cold War was alive and well in the squared circle in those days.

I hadn't heard much about the Sheik during the past couple

of decades, but Twitter was a lifeline to him and he embraced the medium with a fervour and craziness the likes of which may only have been seen by those who were lucky enough to witness Rob Ford attack a pipe. The Iron Sheik may not have actually been running his own Twitter account, but whoever was running it was not afraid to offend. Nothing was off-limits, and one of the Sheik's most frequently used insults involved telling people that he was going to "fuck them in the ass and make them humble." Gay jokes, racist jokes—you name it, the Sheik did it, and a surprising number of people embraced it. People got a kick out of the Sheik following them on Twitter or, better yet, insulting them on Twitter, as was the case with me.

But why the hell was the Iron Sheik's hairy hand squeezing the life out of me that afternoon at the CBC? Turns out Steven Kerzner had read the one chapter in *Anchorboy* where I mentioned that I liked wrestling as a kid, and from there he deduced that it would be a hilarious segment to set me up by having the Sheik surprise me on set. Hey, it was no more crazy than anything else that had happened to me over those two days.

The Sheik shook a delighted George's hand and then shook mine. "Hello, Iron Sheik," I deadpanned.

"Fine," he replied. Okay, then.

"Okay, listen, listen man. I follow you on Twitter and you say all kinds of controversial things. Did you ever take a risk where you think you've gone too far?" asked George, keeping the risk-taking subject going with a determined focus. Say what you will about the guy, but he's a real pro.

And the Sheik replied as only he could:

"I AM TORONTO. AND TODAY I BEEN IN THE MAYOR OFFICE. TODAY THE MISTER MAYOR, YOU SUPPOSED TO BE ROLE MODEL FOR THE TORONTO, CANADA. BUT I

WANT TO SAY, MR. FORD . . . OR MISTER WHATEVER ROB FORD, I WISH YOU CAN COME CHALLENGE . . . WITH ME . . . ARM WRESTLING. OR WRESTLING . . . YEAH! YEAH!"

The Sheik wanted to go on, but George was already getting the "wrap it up" signal from his floor director. He kindly mentioned Emma's upcoming pop culture show, Arthur's upcoming stand-up gigs, and my book, and then the segment was over. The most bizarre television segment in history had come to a close. The Sheik was always up for publicity, but a recent stunt in which Hulk Hogan had arm-wrestled Mayor Ford (and lost) had given him fuel for this ridiculous debacle.

I bid George goodbye, an innocent bystander in all of this, and shook Steven Kerzner's hand and said, "That was weird."

"What, you didn't like it? I thought you'd like it!" he replied.

"It was great! Thanks for having me," I lied. I didn't care anymore. I was done. I was finished with all of this madness.

As we were leaving the CBC in a cab in the pouring rain, one of my publicists told us a story about taking my old Fox Sports 1 pal Regis Philbin around town on a book tour a few years before.

They were in the back of a town car and Regis was on the phone with his wife, Joy. At one point, while listening to Joy talk as he rolled his eyes repeatedly, Regis apparently blurted out: "Baby, we're going into a tunnel! I'm gonna lose you! I'm sorry!" and hung up. There was no tunnel. I laughed pretty hard at that story. There was nothing left to do but laugh at everything that had happened that day.

The previous evening I had my very first ever book signing for *Anchorboy* at the massive two-story Indigo bookstore on the corner of Bay and Bloor in downtown Toronto. When promoting the appearance on my Instagram account I made an off-hand comment that I would bring ketchup chips to the signing for everyone to snack on. "You do realize this means you actually have to bring the chips, don't you?" said my wife's best friend, Christina, upon seeing my Instagram.

She was right.

Luckily my publicist, Kelsey, was more than happy to round up the tasty Canadian snacks for me. When I arrived at the signing she had ten bags of ketchup chips there waiting, and when I walked into the main hall, I handed them out like Robin Hood tossing bags of coins to the poor.

The whole evening went spectacularly well. My friend and former TSN colleague Matt Cauz, co-host of *Macko and Cauz* on TSN Radio, was kind enough to come down and interview me in front of a packed house, and I answered such hard-hitting questions as "Have you been to the Brass Rail strip club since you returned to Toronto?" ("No, but I will go later tonight") and "Why did you leave us and take a job in Los Angeles? ("Money"). I signed books and took pictures for almost two hours, and any bad feelings about the day were swept away.

The next night I did another signing at the Chapters in Etobicoke—the home of, you guessed it, Rob Ford. As promised, my old friend Dana McKiel showed up and waited for two hours until everyone else had gone home. I wasn't mad at Dana or anything; in fact, looking back, the idea that he would crash *The Social* kind of delights me. When it was all over, I realized I had barely eaten all day, so Doug, my editor, put me in a car and we headed back toward the city along Queensway Avenue. Doug wanted to take me to a place he'd been going to for years: Mamma Martino's—just your classic North American Italian red-and-white checkered cloth family-style joint. The food was good, but after those rain-soaked and bizarre days it tasted better than good. I had dreamt of doing my own book tour and I had gotten my wish. Driving back downtown to my hotel after a wonderful meal, I couldn't help but think that the whole experience might make a nice little story for a future book.

Chapter 14

An Eternity in Cottage Country

"Would you like to come up to my cottage for the weekend?"
Are there twelve better words that you could possibly say
to a Canadian?

There doesn't seem to be any real logic to Canadian vernacular
when it comes to vacation properties. For some Atlantic Canadians
and Northern Ontarians the term used is "camp," even if they are
heading to an actual home with four walls and a roof over their
heads. Growing up in Alberta, we called them cabins. And for
Ontario and Quebec it's all about cottage country. Either way we
are all talking about the same thing: taking advantage of the fact
that our country has the most freshwater lakes in the world and
staking our own personal little slice of heaven beside one of them.

A few years ago I started thinking it was time to buy a cottage
of my own. But before I did anything rash, I figured it might be

a good idea to test the waters by renting a place for a week in the summer and doing nothing but sit on the dock, drink Caesars, barbeque, and swim. If I was bored after a week of cottage activity, then maybe it really wasn't a good idea to buy. Or maybe I would love the experience so much I would be convinced to buy right away. The possibilities were very exciting!

I should have just asked around to friends who either had cottages or knew someone who might want to rent one, but instead I went the Kijiji route. For those unfamiliar with Kijiji (Americans), it is essentially Craigslist, but for whatever reason more popular in Canada. There were a ton of places for rent, but eventually I settled on what appeared to be a cute little cottage on Lake Muskoka about two hours north of Toronto. Chobi and I made the trek north on the 400, past Barrie to Muskoka Lake country to begin our cottage adventure.

That's when things started to go wrong.

Somewhat predictably, the place was older and smaller than it had appeared in the preview pictures. But this wasn't a major surprise for me as I already knew that every single vacation place anyone has ever rented online has turned out to be smaller than expected—at the very least. Anyway, the place might be tiny and much closer to the neighbouring cottages than we'd have liked, but it would certainly do for our purposes.

And then we discovered there was no running water.

I thought maybe it was my responsibility to turn on a lever or gauge for a pump somewhere, so I called the real estate agency and they informed me that, no, the cottage should in fact have running water. This was a genuine problem, and we would have to call the cottage owner to come fix said problem. I dialed the number of the cottage owner and he immediately picked up.

"Hi, I'm renting your cottage out in Muskoka," I began.

"Oh, great! How are you enjoying it?" he asked.

"It's just fine other than the fact that we don't seem to have any running water."

"Oh, that's a problem," he said without much emotion.

Unless you want us to take a shit on your kitchen floor! I thought, then said, "Yes, it's a bit of a problem."

"My wife and I just sat down to dinner. It's our anniversary," he stated.

I wasn't sure what to say. That was a real bummer and I obviously didn't want to interrupt their anniversary dinner. At the same time, I had already paid for this cottage, and there was no way we were going to stay there without running water. Or should I say, there was no way *my girlfriend* was going to stay there without running water. Chobi was already busy searching "Muskoka Lakes Area Hotels" on her iPhone.

"I am so sorry to interrupt your dinner"—and I meant it—"but we were told to call this number in case of emergencies. The rental office is already closed for the day. We have absolutely no running water and we paid for the place. I think this qualifies as an emergency."

He sighed a defeated sigh and paused a second before saying, "Okay, I'll be right out." Ugh, sorry dude.

Not surprisingly, at this point the concept of renting out a cottage that I owned in order to cover the taxes and costs of upkeep started to seem less appealing. I could just imagine myself out for dinner with Chobi at our favourite restaurant, several drinks in, only to get a call from some disgruntled couple because the cottage stove didn't work, and could I come out and fix it, and no I don't know how to fix a stove. The realities of cottage ownership were starting to set in. The previous summer, I had witnessed my friend Rob spend a good portion of the time he had at his wife's cottage at

Stoney Lake in the Kawartha Lakes region re-shingling the entire cottage by himself with his own two hands. I asked him if he was left with an incredible sense of accomplishment after maintaining and fixing the cottage all by himself. I wondered if there was some sort of sense of manliness that came from doing it on your own. But when he answered, "If I could do it all over again, I would just pay someone else to do it and relax on the dock," I honestly wasn't that surprised.

Chobi and I sat drinking the wine and eating the cheese we had brought up from Toronto, forgetting the fact that when the cottage owner said he'd be right up, he meant in approximately two hours.

When he finally arrived things had taken a turn for the worse as the whole area was in the early stages of a heavy downpour. The owner of the cottage was absolutely massive, and I mean fat. There's really no other way to describe the guy. I felt uncomfortable just looking at him. I felt even more uncomfortable when he determined that it was indeed part of an ongoing problem: A lot of leaves and seaweed had been gathering near the shore at his cottage, and as a result the water system that pulled from the lake was completely clogged. The poor guy was going to have to wade into the water and unclog everything by hand. By the time he had come to this realization the rain was coming down hard. We're talking Biblical hard, "the Bishop having the best game of his life" in *Caddyshack* hard—so hard that he had a tough time just opening the shed to find his hip-waders so he could wander out into the lake. Waiting until the rain died down was simply not an option. This man had an anniversary dinner to get to! By the time he drove out to meet us, fixed the water system, and drove back it would be a total of five hours. I'm pretty sure when he walked in the front door of his Markham home later that night his wife would be long gone.

The whole process took an hour. I watched the man the whole

time but could offer little help. Well, in hindsight, I suppose I could have joined him and stood waist-deep naked in the rain, but I was on vacation. Instead, Chobi and I stayed dry in the comfort of this man's tiny cottage while he unclogged the pipes handful by disgusting handful. Eventually, he waded back to shore, took off the hip-waders, and came back inside absolutely soaking wet. We tried the tap, and after a few gasps and wheezes it sputtered to life and out came relatively clean water that we would use for nothing else but shitting and showering. He apologized for the pipes, we apologized for ruining his anniversary, and we all said an uncomfortable goodbye before he stumbled back to his sedan soaking wet for what was likely an even more uncomfortable two-hour ride home. This was cottage ownership.

The next day we awoke to sweet Ontario sunshine that made the previous evening seem like a bad dream. We were determined not to let our bad start ruin our entire week's vacation, so after coffee on the dock—one of the very best parts of being at a cottage or cabin— we relaxed in a set of Muskoka chairs (Adirondack chairs to you non-Ontarians) with books we hadn't even cracked the spines on yet. After about an hour of peaceful reading we heard laughing and screaming from the cottage next door, then witnessed a group of younger adults, five guys and five girls, no older than twenty-four, all pile into a large cabin cruiser boat and take off down the lake to spend the day tubing and wakeboarding. Good, I thought, those rabble-rousers are out of our hair for the day and we can relax! How old was I getting anyway?

That evening, I was excited about barbequing; I love to fire up the barbeque and grill. Such a cliché. Man, fire, food. I buy into it wholeheartedly. When it comes to men and grilling I am happy to live and eat the stereotype. I had a couple of beautiful steaks from Sanagan's butcher shop in Kensington Market and potatoes sliced and patted with butter, salt, pepper, and green onions that I had wrapped in tinfoil. Chobi was putting together a Caesar salad in the cottage kitchen. It was such a pleasure to be cooking with her just by ourselves and away from everything in the city. Maybe we just needed a few days to acclimate to the surroundings. The gang of twenty-somethings next door was having fun, but not in a disrespectful way—we had no complaints about the neighbours, however close in proximity they may have been. The sun was going down and it was beautiful. It was one of those idyllic Muskoka sunsets you hear about, as if this natural wonder alone was reason enough to rake two yards of leaves, mow two laws, re-shingle two roofs. All the practical arguments for *not* owning a cottage—the extra work, the hassle, the taxes—they just melt away with your first look at a Muskoka sunset. That's what they say anyway, and they may very well be right.

Then I fired up the barbeque.

At least, I *tried*.

I should first point out that this wasn't exactly a normal barbeque—more like a hibachi on a wobbly set of legs with a propane tank propped somewhat dangerously underneath on the ground. I twisted open the gas on the propane tank, and using a long wooden match I made a feeble attempt to poke the long stick into the top of the grill and fire up the cooking contraption. First attempt unsuccessful. I tried lighting another match. Still no go. As dumb as I am, even I knew this was the time to shut off the propane and let it dissipate a bit before giving it another try. What if I couldn't get this barbeque going? Was I going to have to cook all this delicious food on an old cottage stove? The horror!

I waited a few more seconds, then cranked on the propane tank again. I tentatively lit another long matchstick, covered my eyes, reached out my arm, and gingerly tried to mate gas and flame. What happened next could best be described as a towering fireball in the night sky. A flame shot straight up into the air like I had set off the pyrotechnic show at a Monster Truck rally. I looked around to see if anyone had witnessed my attempt at singeing off my own eyebrows and face, but thankfully the party next door was already in full swing and they certainly weren't interested in the comings and goings of the renters next door. It's a good thing. We were clearly out of our element up here.

Once satisfied that I hadn't suffered any third-degree burns, I peered into the grill and discovered that despite the fact that I nearly re-enacted Michael Jackson's Pepsi commercial from the '80s where he lost half his scalp, the barbeque was only half lit. Or should I say there was only a flame flickering on one side of the tiny contraption. The other side was still as dark and cold as the lake. The listing on the cottage rental said, "BBQ." I took this brief description to mean "working barbeque." I guess I should have inquired to see if that barbeque wasn't a death trap that would heat only a portion of the grill big enough to cook one small sliced zucchini. I threw the potatoes on top of the tiny flickering flame. At this rate they would be ready in two days. The steaks, seasoned with salt and pepper and olive oil, and practically begging to be thrown on top of hot iron, sat there pathetically doing nothing.

Then the shitstorm arrived—an absolute shitstorm of mosquitoes.

Now, I have had some experience living in parts of Canada that were badly infested with mosquitoes: my family's summer cabin on Baptiste Lake near my hometown; summer nights on golf courses in Athabasca; the entire city of Winnipeg. In Athabasca "lake country," much like lake country all across Canada, you basically have four months to use your cabin, cottage, or camp. This is limiting enough, but then consider the fact that in most parts of Canada those four months are interrupted by about eight weeks of heavy mosquito infestation.

I remember following my last year of high school a couple of guys in town decided to start renting "soft-sider" hot tubs that they would bring to your lake cabin and set up for you. It was all the rage in the County of Athabasca in the summer of 1992. One weekend my parents decided they had better start spending some nights out at the cabin so I convinced them it would be a good idea to rent one of these soft-siders that the whole family and their friends could enjoy. We invited some store employees, and my sister and I each had a few friends over. We fired up the barbeque and started grilling, and we had plenty of Kokanee on ice. Even though the mosquitoes were biting they weren't *too* bad, and we were all kind of looking at each other thinking the same thing: *We have our own getaway cabin; we need to be here more often.*

Then the sun went down.

The soft-sider hot tub had been filled up and heated sufficiently that we could all jump in. Probably a dozen or so people just squished into this oversized kiddie pool. No one cared. This was great! Until that fatal moment when the mosquitoes really started to emerge.

The sun had gone down and this was their time to feast. Suddenly, those of us whose shoulders were exposed were jolting and swatting every couple of seconds, desperately trying to keep the bugs at bay. It was no use. People started to flee back to the cabin, and the rest of us who decided to tough it out were forced to submerge ourselves in the water so that nothing was exposed but our eyes and forehead. If someone had walked up to us at that moment they would have thought we were a theatre group all doing impressions of Marlon Brando as Colonel Kurtz in the climactic scene of *Apocalypse Now.*

Point is: I know mosquitoes and how to deal with them.

But these mosquitoes were different. They were positively relentless. I thought maybe if I stood close to the tiny, flickering flame underneath the grill the little skeeters might be scared off, but I was terribly mistaken. The sun had set, and in the dark of night on the edge of the lake it was feeding time. Swatting and slapping like a total idiot, I was getting attacked on all fronts and there was no letting up. Chobi came outside to check on me, and they pounced on her like she was a baby deer in the forest who had wandered into a wolf's den. "What the hell?" she screamed and ran back into the cottage, slamming the fragile screen door behind her. I grabbed the uncooked steaks, twisted off the gas on the propane tank, used tongs to lift the barely warm potatoes off the grill, and fought through a haze of bugs in the ten or so steps to that fragile screen door, which we proceeded to keep closed for the remainder of the night, quietly munching on our Caesar salads and wondering if uncooked potatoes might satisfy the hordes of bloodthirsty insects outside.

The next morning we made a very important decision.

We woke up, had one last coffee on the dock, and then packed up all the food—cooked, uncooked, and otherwise—as well as the remaining wine and vodka we thought we'd need to keep us buzzed for an entire week, and stuffed it all into the trunk of my car along with our clothes. We locked up the cottage and tore out of the driveway. Almost at the turn to the main road, we saw the kids from next door all gathered at the back of their cottage, preparing their wetsuits and wakeboards for another day in paradise in the Canadian wilderness.

"Where are you guys going?" asked an affable young man who had clearly grown up spending every summer happily frolicking at this cottage, first with his family and now with his friends, his skin probably leathery from adapting to the myriad of mosquito attacks he had endured since he was a boy.

"I just don't think this was the place for us," I said before bidding him a warm goodbye and driving off.

We dropped the keys in an envelope and then left them in the mailbox of the rental agency in the middle of town, keeping the engine running the entire time. We were a bit anxious to get to our next destination and we kept driving. We knew exactly where we needed to go. We got back on the 400, then onto the 401, and passed Number 9 Channel Nine Court in Scarborough, the home of TSN. We kept driving past the eastern suburbs of the city, past the Big Apple stand on the side of the highway where they sold the most delicious apple pies, and then through beautiful Prince Edward County near Kingston a couple hours later. Prince Edward County is Ontario's new wine country—Ontario's version of the Hamptons—and we love going there, but that wasn't where we needed to be now.

We kept driving past Cornwall, over the Quebec border, and then finally reached the outskirts of our destination.

Beautiful Montreal.

There are so many amazing cities in my home country. Toronto will always feel like home to me. As will Edmonton. Winnipeg is an unexpected treasure, and I have friends there I will cherish for life. I never have a bad time in Saskatoon or Halifax. But Montreal tops them all. Everything about the city puts me at ease. I could live there at a moment's notice. And this week, even though we had pre-paid for a cottage that was now going to sit empty for the next six days, Montreal's sweet embrace was going to make us forget all about that poor man who had to come all the way from Markham and been forced to abandon his anniversary dinner, all about the mosquitoes and the world's worst barbeque.

We drove through the city, through Montreal's *centre-ville*, and past office buildings and *Couche-Tards* and St. Hubert chicken restaurants, until we finally arrived at our destination: Boulevard Saint Laurent. "The Main." We pulled into the newly refurbished and mercifully modern and clean Opus Hotel at the corner of St. Laurent and Sherbrooke and were immediately greeted by a smiling porter who took our bags and led us to the front desk. We were given a beautiful room overlooking the street with a shower big enough for two that we may have lingered in for over an hour.

Filth and memories of the past two days washed away, we left the car with the valet and hopped into a cab to Montreal's Atwater neighbourhood and my favourite restaurant in the entire nation— and perhaps the whole world—Joe Beef. The tiny little bistro owned by friends and co-head chefs David McMillan and Frederic Morin had taken the city's food scene by storm and charmed the likes of Anthony Bourdain and David Chang. We squeezed into a tiny wooden table, the entire place absolutely rammed, and ordered the first of many wonderfully made cocktails before I tucked into my appetizer, the Foie Gras Double Down, a takeoff on the KFC sandwich of the same name. In KFC's version, the sandwich "bread" is two pieces of chicken breast. Joe Beef's version uses two thick slabs of foie gras—foie gras to envelop the sandwich! This over-the-top indulgence, followed by a spectacular and fully cooked steak that enjoyed the kiss of real flames instead of a tiny flickering one, was more than enough to restore mind and body on that beautiful summer night. We passed out on 300-thread-count sheets that night, and as Chobi slumbered beside me in peaceful bliss I stared up at the ceiling.

I had wanted to spend the entirety of that evening on the dock with a drink in hand, taking in the spectacular Muskoka night sky filled with stars. Now I was still staring upwards, but the sky was obscured by a newly spackled and gleaming white ceiling. I was staring into nothingness, and I cracked a little smile. We had found our dream cottage after all.

Chapter 15

A Night Out in the San Fernando Valley

B y the time I moved to Los Angeles I was ready to visit all the places I had heard and read about: the beaches at Malibu, the Laurel Canyon neighbourhood where so many musical icons had lived during the late 1960s and early '70s, and of course the San Fernando Valley where all the greatest adult films in the world were made. There was no "Porn Disneyland" where one could go and learn more about the history of the genre, just a massive suburban sprawl hiding its secrets carefully.

My friend Ben Zigelstein, who directed studio shows for TSN, came down to L.A. just a few months after we moved there to visit his screenwriter brother and messaged me about getting together. I told him I wanted to visit a strip club in the Valley when a porn star was dancing there. I wanted to see the Valley in person and I wanted to see a porn star up close—a real live porn star in the ultimate porn

169

star habitat. As luck would have it, the week Ben was visiting a porn star *was* going to be dancing at a club in the Valley. The porn star in question was Kristina Rose, a beautiful, petite Latina behind whose innocent smile lurked a foul mouth that made even me blush. I imagined she would have a tremendously entertaining stage presence. I don't think it's what Ben had in mind when he asked me if I wanted to go out for a drink that evening, but I was pretty confident that even if the night turned out to be a total disaster we would have a good time. It *was* a strip club after all.

My wife approved the outing on the condition that I took another female friend along. Julie Stewart Binks worked alongside me at Fox Sports 1 after spending the first portion of her on-air career at CTV Regina. Julie was always up for fun, and when I mentioned to her that I wanted to go to a strip club in the Valley she didn't even bat an eyelash. So after a delicious meal at Petty Cash Taqueria on Beverly Boulevard near La Brea, we hopped into an Uber Black Car and began the trip "over the hill." Normally, anyone familiar with Los Angeles might say to themselves, "Isn't an Uber from Hollywood to the Valley a little expensive?" And they would be absolutely correct. But having just arrived in the city on a work visa, I didn't want to risk any possibility whatsoever of getting caught with a DUI—a little extra money for the Uber would be worth it.

After heading up the 101 we exited on Sepulveda near Ventura Boulevard in Van Nuys. "It looks like Regina," commented Julie.

We drove down a pretty dark stretch of Oxnard right next to a Costco en route to the Spearmint Rhino, a chain of strip clubs with locations all over Los Angeles and a famous branch in Vegas. Having really only been to American strip clubs in Vegas, I was curious to see how this club in the Valley stacked up—pardon the pun.

We pulled up to the front door and were asked for a $20 cover, which seemed fair enough. I paid quickly, excited to step inside, get a drink, and check out the action. The three of us wandered up to the bar and asked for some vodka and we got a look that said, "Don't you realize you can't order booze here?"

We did *not* realize you couldn't order booze there.

Have you ever been to a strip club? Have you ever been to one completely, 100 percent sober? There's a difference. There's a *big* difference. No matter what you think of strip clubs, I think we can all agree that alcohol should probably be available. Without alcohol, it was a little like watching girls dance at a dimly lit Starbucks that happened to smell like really, really cheap perfume and a smattering of broken dreams. The club was not quite dark enough either, just a little *too* bright. Despite all these obstacles, we decided to sit on "pervert's row" right in front of the stage. And a tiny stage it was. At the world-famous Brass Rail strip club in Toronto the stage is rectangular and features two poles for maximum movement and dexterity. By comparison, this stage was tiny, which meant the performers were literally right in your face. I suppose that was the point.

As we walked in I saw Kristina Rose standing at one of the back booths with a ton of her merchandise arranged on the table for sale. This "merchandise" consisted of signed posters and DVDs, as well as signed boxes that contained pocket vaginas, which were replicas of Kristina's own vagina made of rubber that could be taken home and used for reasons I'm still very much unclear on, despite my years of watching adult films. Do you put the rubber vagina on the bed and then get on top to penetrate it? Do you lie on your back and then secure the rubber vagina on top of your erection like a floppy hat at the beach? I can't imagine any situation in which a man using one of Kristina's rubber vaginas wouldn't look completely hilarious to someone who happened to barge in and catch him in the act. Nonetheless, Kristina had sold a few of those vaginas that evening, as well as a ton of pics. She was smiling and seemed happy. I didn't approach her right away for fear of looking like the kind of guy who took an Uber all the way to the Valley just to see her, even though I *had* just taken an Uber all the way to the Valley just to see her.

As it turns out, I wasn't alone.

There were various characters joining us on pervert's row surrounding the tiny stage that Saturday evening, and most of them seemed pretty sober. Directly next to us sat a young guy, early twenties, who had a stack of one-dollar bills ready to shower on Kristina so she would shake her booty directly in front of him. I imagined that this kid was a lot like me. He had probably gone to a sleepover with his friends when he was about twelve years old and someone had a laptop and showed him a pornographic movie for the first time and he became hooked. Why else would he be here all alone on a Saturday night, unless he was just plain anti-social? In my sober state I was a little sad that this young guy was sitting in the front row with us and not out at a club with friends meeting real girls and having a good time. He looked completely tense and I wished I could've bought him a shot to loosen him up a bit, but I obviously couldn't, and that would have been a bit creepy anyway. Besides, I had already established my creepy bonafides by showing up to this joint in the first place.

Next to the young kid sat the kind of couple I imagined lived all over the San Fernando Valley. The guy looked like a classic California beach bum, mid- to late forties, long blond hair, a shirt cut off at the sleeves, and pale blue jeans with high-top sneakers. He had several bracelets around his wrist, a couple of shell necklaces, and earrings in both ears. For all I knew he was a pimp, or Kristina's manager, or maybe he just pumped gas at that Costco next door. Either way, he had a much younger girl with him who appeared to have been briefed about the no-alcohol policy at the club and had taken the necessary steps beforehand to ensure she did not show up sober to the proceedings. She had on a dirty T-shirt and jeans, and her hair was pulled up in a ponytail. She could have been a runaway or a potential porn-star-in-waiting, or she was simply sitting next to her dad, who had brought her here because he had custody for the weekend.

Then there was Eric Duhatschek.

Not the *real* Eric Duhatschek, longtime sportswriter for one of Canada's national newspapers, the *Globe and Mail*, who hailed from Calgary. Knowing Eric even just a little, I figured he was probably not the kind of guy I would find in a place like this. And besides, the Flames weren't in town that weekend. This guy did, however, bear an uncanny resemblance to the respected hockey scribe: thin, glasses, balding; he also looked just a smidge like the Nazi whose face melts off at the end of *Raiders of the Lost Ark*. There was no real reason for me to pay any special attention to this man, but something about him set me off right away. He was sitting at the far side of the stage from us, directly next to the stage door so he would be the first to see Kristina saunter out into the spotlight.

More importantly, he came bearing gifts.

He had actual presents for Kristina: two large gift bags that sat on the chair beside him, a chair that would otherwise have gone unoccupied. By the look of things, it appeared that the guy had brought clothes or possibly even lingerie. I couldn't make out the name of the store on either bag, but it's safe to say he had brought along something he hoped Kristina would wear for him in a private setting or perhaps just take a picture of herself wearing and send to him so he could keep it close by on the nightstand. He stared straight ahead and said nothing, a Coke in front of him barely touched. Julie asked me why I was so preoccupied with the guy, and the only answer I could muster was that he was going to be competing with me for this former porn star's attention and he had come prepared with a more impressive arsenal. I was so ill-prepared that I didn't even have any one-dollar bills in my pocket to shower on Kristina when she eventually arrived on stage. I think I was a little gun shy after all my strip club experiences in Alberta.

As I explained to my friends that evening, in Alberta the strip clubs were pretty much the same as they were all across Canada, save for one notable exception: Instead of showering the girls with one-dollar bills like they did in the U.S. or just sitting there indifferently like they did in Ontario or Quebec, the standard and accepted practice was to *throw loonies on stage at the girls while they danced.* I will give you a moment to go back and read that sentence again because I'm sure if you haven't been to an Alberta strip club you might be in shock. But that's not even the half of it. Not only were you encouraged to throw heavy one-dollar coins in the direction of dancing women like they were some sort of attraction in the circus, you were encouraged by the girls themselves to aim the loonies directly at their vaginas.

Directly at their vaginas.

Sometimes strippers would hold 8-by-10 photos of themselves up to their vaginas to give patrons a larger target. As far as I know this is still standard practice in Alberta strip clubs and obviously began when Canada switched from one-dollar bills to one-dollar coins in 1987. In the U.S. they're still using paper money, and I'm sure it's appreciated by the ladies on stage.

Back in the Valley, the dancers came out one by one—the warm-up acts, if you will. There was the skinny blonde with no breasts and the curvy brunette with fake breasts; all of them seemed pretty indifferent to us sitting and staring at them, and with no alcohol to loosen up the patrons the entire thing was truly depressing. "I hope Kristina is next," I kept saying to Ben and Julie, but time after time I was disappointed as the curtain opened to reveal another Angelino vixen. We had consumed several drinks at Petty Cash, but the booze had worn off and now I had deep regrets about dragging my two friends along to witness this depressing spectacle.

And then out of the corner of my eye I spotted Kristina hurriedly making her way through the club to the backstage area. Five minutes of giddy anticipation later it was show time. The first few beats of "Let Me Blow Ya Mind" by Eve and Gwen Stefani blasted over the club's PA system, and the strip club DJ, perhaps the most noble of all professions, allowed his smooth and assured voice to permeate the evening.

"Laaaadies and gentlemennn . . . it's time for your headliner. Please welcome to the stage . . . the star of adult films for Wicked Pictures, Vivid Pictures, Evil Angel, Elegant Angel, and more . . . All the way from the San Fernando Valley to the San Fernando Valley . . . it's Kristina Rose!"

Then the curtain opened.

The crowd was suddenly brought to life by the sight of this four-foot-eleven manic-pixie dream girl with brown hair and a killer smile. Kristina's energy was off the charts, and she came out screaming and skipping and rustling up everyone's hair and generally turning a dud of an evening into a great one. Before you say "it must be the cocaine," Kristina has sworn in interviews that she doesn't touch the stuff, while admitting to being the world's biggest pothead this side of Snoop Dogg. Not sure if I believed her or not but I was damn sure I didn't care. It wasn't as if I was lusting after this woman, I was just in awe of her full commitment to the task at hand. The club wasn't full—far from it—it was actually mostly empty, but Kristina made it feel like *the* place to be that night. At that moment, she was a true entertainer.

And there she was, paying *way* too much attention to Eric Duhatschek.

She spent time with everyone around pervert's row, but since I had no one-dollar bills to shower on her, she politely moved on to the May-to-December L.A. couple who seemed to have an endless supply tucked into their pockets and literally made them rain on her as she shook her ample booty. The young guy who arrived by himself got plenty of attention too. Then it was back to Duhatschek again and finally to the pole, which she worked like a pro. My mouth was open the entire time. What a rank amateur I was, just sitting there with my friends like an idiot.

When Kristina was finished, she disappeared backstage and I thought she was done for the evening, but just a few minutes later she returned to the table at the back to hawk more of her merchandise.

"Go chat with her, get a picture," said Julie and Ben.

"Why not?" I thought, as I tried to casually speed-walk my way to the back of the club where Kristina was chatting with—you guessed it—Eric Duhatschek.

I couldn't believe this imposter had out-creeped me and managed to get to the front of the line first. Okay, truthfully there wasn't actually a line. It was just me and him. Rather, it was just Kristina talking to Duhatschek, with me standing behind them like the creepiest human who ever walked the face of the planet Earth. *I should be home drinking a beer in front of the TV watching* Saturday Night Live *right now*, I thought. What the hell possessed me to chase after some bizarre teenage fantasy about meeting one of my favourite porn stars? I was a happily married man for Christ's sake! Did I think Kristina was going to fall in love with me on the spot and ask me to take her away from this seedy world? Not to mention the fact that I had directed an inordinate amount of vitriol at a man who was probably just lonely and wanted to bask in the affections of a girl who was more than happy to take his gifts and probably his money. No harm was really being done here. I suddenly felt a whole lot of shame, and I decided to turn around, gather my friends, and Uber us all back to Hollywood so I could find a proper bar to buy them a few drinks and forget this whole trip to the Valley ever happened.

Then I heard Kristina say, "Hey, where ya going?"

I turned around and she was smiling at me. I wasn't going anywhere.

What does one say the first time he meets a porn star?

"Hi!" a little too eagerly.

"Hi!" she said back. "What's your name?"

"I'm Jay," I said. "You were great up there."

"Thanks! Where you from? You're cute!" She knew all the lines.

"I just moved here. I'm a sportscaster!" Like she gave a shit.

"Really? That's awesome! Do you like L.A.?"

I replied that I really, *really* liked L.A.

What followed was some small talk that I was terrible at, but like any woman who had probably spent her entire working life making men feel comfortable in her presence, she made me feel like I was the smartest and best looking guy in the room. And like so many men before me, I fell for everything, stopping short of purchasing the Kristina Rose pocket vagina but forking over money for a signed 8 by 10 and then finding it impossible not to grin from ear to ear as she offered to take a picture with me.

"Grab my ass!" she said. And I did. Chobi would not be thrilled when she saw the picture but, you know, when in Rome.

She hugged me goodbye and then moved on to the next customer. She had pocket replicas of her reproductive organs to sell!

I thought Kristina Rose was terrific. She was a hustler, and like all adult film stars I worried about the circumstances that led her to this profession. But she was practical and real, and when it came to dealing with guys like me, she could have taught a lot of people who run businesses a thing or two about customer service. She had told me she wasn't doing porn anymore, just snapchats and Skype chats with guys on her computer for money. And of course, there was the dancing. The business had become "too sketchy," she said. I wondered how many adult film stars had uttered those words upon leaving the business. She sounded like a veteran of any industry who, with the benefit of experience, could see things for what they really were. I hope everything worked out for her.

The drive home was pretty fun. We all agreed that none of us would ever return to this particular establishment again, much less this part of L.A. We had seen everything we needed to see here. I had broken the myth of adult film stars. My friends had humoured my little adventure. It was time for some late-night whiskey. My treat.

Chapter 16

Things Get Messy

Presidents of major sports networks in both the United States and Canada probably spend a good 37 percent of their day taking ticket requests for sporting events from clients and employees. I am actually amazed how cool they always seem about it. My standard answer in that situation would be "I'm trying to run a major sports network here. Maybe get out your credit card and go buy tickets yourself, you pale, gangly wart." Or something to that effect.

That said, a few months after moving to L.A., I ran into Fox Sports president Eric Shanks in our building on the 21st Century Fox lot, and after he asked how my wife and I were settling in to Los Angeles, I asked this question:

"Eric, my wife is a huge UFC fan. Any chance you would have access to a pair of tickets to UFC 167 this weekend? I'm happy to pay for them."

"You don't have to pay for them," Eric replied with a laugh. "How bloody do you want to get?"

How bloody do you want to get? God, I love working for this company.

I wasn't lying when I said Chobi was a huge UFC fan. She's the person who turned me on to the UFC. Like a lot of boxing fans who grew up with that sport, I was dismissive of mixed martial arts as either barbaric or boring, or both. My argument was always the same: For every UFC pay-per-view event I'd seen, one good fight would be marred by four bad fights that involved two men in short-shorts hugging each other on the ground like a toddler smothering his teddy bear.

But soon after Chobi and I started dating she took a trip to Vegas with friends and got tickets to UFC 100 (through the president of TSN, of course). She came back telling tales of sequin-clad women ringside and an amazing crowd at the MGM Grand Garden Arena. So I decided to give the sport another shot. A regular routine for us wild ones on a Saturday night would be to order up the latest UFC pay-per-view, grab some Hot 'n' Spicy from Popeyes chicken, and watch grown men and women beat the living crap out of each other.

So now that I was working for Fox—the UFC's primary American broadcaster—I had access to all of this carnage in the flesh. With *extra bloody* UFC 167 tickets secured from my very kind employer, we booked a quick flight to Vegas for the weekend. I was about to experience my first MMA pay-per-view event in person.

Side note: One of the underrated bonuses of moving to Los Angeles? It's a one-hour flight to Las Vegas. I know plenty of people enjoy the drive, but once you live through the experience of leaving your home in L.A. and then checking in to your Las Vegas hotel *exactly* three hours later (door to door), it's difficult to get in your vehicle and go back down that highway. I love Vegas, but two days is perfect for me. In Canada a four-day trip was the standard based on all the charter flights. You either flew down on a Thursday and returned on a Sunday or vice versa. For me, the old Canadian four-day trip was always a bit *too much* fun. Days one and two were always an all-night blast, day three was subdued by two straight hangovers, and day four was a flat-out writeoff. By the time I reached the end of a four-day Vegas trip, I was always convinced I was going to shit myself on the flight home because of alcohol poisoning.

That evening, Chobi and I put on the closest things either of us owned to a sequined dress (her) and an Affliction T-shirt and bedazzled jeans (me) and we walked across the Strip to the MGM for the fight. The main event that night featured Canadian Georges St-Pierre against bearded Texan upstart Johny Hendricks for the UFC welterweight title. A native of Montreal, St-Pierre was the undisputed star of the sport. With three welterweight championships to his name, this fight seemed like another easy challenge for a guy who'd once been a bouncer at a night club called Fuzzy.

A month previously Dan and I had been hired by the good folks at Coca-Cola—makers of NOS energy drink—to accompany a group of contest winners to St-Pierre's gym in Montreal for a training and workout session. St-Pierre's manager had told the Coca-Cola executives that the mostly affable St-Pierre hated only two things in life:

1. Meeting people
2. Speaking English

Dan and I were hired to serve as a buffer between the champ and the contest winners and to help break the ice. We were paid handsomely for our efforts, but really, anytime someone invites us to Montreal we go regardless of the gig because it is quite simply one of the greatest cities on planet Earth. As it turned out, Georges's English was just fine, probably better than ours, and if he really didn't enjoy meeting the contest winners he certainly hid it very well. The group consisted of about ten people who were each allowed to bring along a friend or loved one. Georges put us through our paces at the gym, taking us step by step through several wrestling moves and even demonstrating some real grappling with his coach and sensei. It was hilarious to watch everyone beg Georges to "put them out" after he demonstrated the sleeper hold. One by one Georges would get behind his guests and twist their arm around so that the person was inadvertently applying pressure on the blood vessels in the neck that allowed oxygen to flow to the brain. (Georges only did it for a second each time, so no one actually collapsed in a heap on the mat.) The whole spectacle was like watching kids in a kindergarten class wait their turn for a ride at the amusement park. "Do me next, Champ! Do me!"

That evening in Las Vegas a month later was expected to be just another token title defence for St-Pierre, who at that point was considered pretty much unbeatable. Johny Hendricks was known as a tough Texas kid who could really take and throw a punch but was also considered a serious underdog against the seasoned MMA veteran. We enjoyed a nice dinner at L'Atelier De Joël Robuchon at the MGM Grand before making our way to the Grand Garden Arena where so many amazing boxing and UFC pay-per-view events had taken place over the years. On our way to the arena, wandering through the MGM casino, it was fascinating to see how this resort had aged so quickly. Once it was considered one of the hottest properties on the strip, but that was when Vegas had just started its mega development of grand new resorts and now it had long been surpassed by other newer, bigger, and more fashionable places. But what really caught our attention was the ridiculously frequent sighting of pairs of dudes wearing full Georges St-Pierre karate gear. In the casino. Without irony. They were on their way to cheer for the champ, and they wanted to look like him too. It was frankly hilarious.

"If Georges actually saw all these guys, he would point and laugh," said Chobi. She was probably right. He would also probably shout something insulting toward them *en français* that they would richly deserve.

We wandered into the arena and found our way to our seats. Eric Shanks wasn't kidding when he asked how bloody we wanted to get. We were sitting two rows away from the octagon. I could have stretched out and touched the shiny shaved head of former *Fear Factor* host Joe Rogan, who was now as well known for being a UFC commentator as Georges St-Pierre was for being an MMA fighter. When I realized my wife was actually very serious about being an MMA fan and insisted on spending several Saturday nights watching UFC pay-per-view events, the most shocking development to me was the fact that Rogan was providing the colour commentary for the sport. "The janitor from *Newsradio*?" I mused. It didn't take him long to prove me to be a fool for ever doubting him. Rogan is just outstanding at his job and knows the sport inside and out, so much so that like all great colour commentators he is able to predict moves and strategies in the ring before they actually happen.

Sitting directly in front of us was the wife of Chael Sonnen, UFC middleweight and frequent analyst on our Fox Sports 1 UFC coverage. Chael was scheduled to fight friend and fellow middleweight Rashad Evans that evening in the fight right before the main event. I first became aware of Chael when he threw his microphone and stormed off the set during a satellite interview on TSN's *Off the Record with Michael Landsberg*. Imagine my surprise when I met Chael and he told me that he and Landsberg had actually become good friends. It wasn't so much that Chael was putting on an act; he is just very, very good at promoting himself. In person, away from the camera, he is actually a soft-spoken, thoughtful, and extremely intelligent guy. That's not to say he isn't intelligent in the octagon, though. After beating Mauricio "Shogun" Rua in a UFC on Fox event on the very first night Fox Sports 1 went on the air, he grabbed the mic seconds after being announced the winner. Exhausted, sweaty—a mess, really—he proceeded to promote UFC's upcoming coverage on Fox Sports 1. I had no idea how he had the presence of mind to gather his thoughts and speak in such an elegant and coherent fashion just *seconds* after giving and taking punches in front of thousands of people, but that's the same reason he was able to serve as a UFC commentator one week and then fight the next. The guy was a real pro. Unfortunately, less than a year later he was out of the sport entirely for failing multiple drug tests and basically humiliating himself. Maybe he wasn't so intelligent after all.

Facing Rashad Evans, Chael was the underdog that evening. Still, nothing prepared us for what happened when the two actually stepped into the ring. Chael was coming off a win and had a little momentum going in, but if Chael's fans had left their seats to go to the bathroom for the first round they would have missed the fight completely. About twenty seconds in Chael was being pummelled on the ground by Evans. I couldn't help but turn my eyes to Chael's wife, who was screaming bloody murder right in front of us. "GET UP! GET UP! GET UP!" she cried. I could only imagine how horrifying this must be for her. Each and every time Chael got into the octagon there was a chance of serious injury, and now he was taking a severe beating from his friend right in front of her eyes. This was his job, and she knew what she was getting into, but she was clearly shaken up when the referees stopped the fight before the first round was over. The entire arena seemed to be stunned at what they had just witnessed. Could Chael have been injured? Or just outclassed? How to explain this one-sided massacre?

I was horrified that Mrs. Sonnen had to witness her husband face an epic beatdown, even though, based on Chael's record, she was probably used to that kind of thing. I turned to Chobi and promised her, right then and there, that she would never see me make a mess of myself like that in front of her at any point during our marriage.

As we waited for the main event, UFC president Dana White wandered over to our seats to say hello. "Having fun?" he asked, while warmly shaking my hand and then moving on to the other people in my row, all of whom were more important to the success of his sport than I. Arnold Schwarzenegger was sitting a few seats to our left, and when he got up to take a Terminator-sized pee he shook hands and greeted people like he was still running for California governor. Arnie: still got it.

Finally, it was time for the main event, and Johny Hendricks entered the ring to a chorus of boos and country music. The crowd was decidedly on the side of the champ, and this guy was to be nothing more than a footnote in the great fighting history of GSP. Soon after, the booming bass and heavy beats of "Man Ah Bad Man" by T.O.K. began to play and out came Georges in his traditional karate outfit and headband. The fight that took place once announcer Bruce Buffer had finished his introductions shocked everyone much more than any Chael Sonnen beatdown ever could.

GSP took a pummelling. It was obvious to anyone watching that he lost the fight. Hendricks took everything St-Pierre could dish out and returned fire with heavy, heavy punches that rocked the champ and hurt him like he had never been hurt before. The whole time, Chobi was on the edge of her seat cheering St-Pierre on, and when he was announced the winner at the end of the fight she pumped her fist with a triumphant "Yes!" never caring for a second whether the decision was fair or not, just relieved that her MMA hero had prevailed and was still officially the champ. It was very similar to the way she cheers for her beloved Toronto Maple Leafs. When your favourite team hasn't won a Stanley Cup since the league expanded from six teams, you don't spend a lot of time worrying about the subtleties of "good" wins versus "bad" ones.

After returning to our hotel that night, I tried to distract myself by checking my losses at the Sports Book, but I just couldn't get the image of a screaming Mrs. Sonnen out of my head.

Back home in Santa Monica the next day, we saw that the apartment next to us had a collection of white sheets of paper plastered to the door. I had noticed one sheet of paper a week before and now it looked like someone had added enough to make a short story. Unable to contain my curiosity, I snuck over to the door and with Chobi protesting read the words on the paper that had been taped there. In summary, the person living in this apartment had failed to pay his rent for two months and these taped sheets of paper were eviction threats. I had seen the guy who lived there once or twice: blond hair, about my age, very quiet. We didn't hear a word out of him. Now it appeared he was a little short of funds, or perhaps just skipping out on the whole "pay rent to live in your apartment" thing, and it wouldn't be long until we had a new neighbour.

The next day I took Chobi to her favourite burger place in Los Angeles for lunch: Plan Check. The restaurant was on Sawtelle Boulevard on the border of Santa Monica and Brentwood, on a street informally known as "Little Osaka" that featured a myriad of Asian restaurants, mostly Japanese. Plan Check stood out as something different. This was a premium but casual burger joint and we loved hitting it up. The kind of place that pretty much insisted on cooking your hamburger medium-rare and you felt like an idiot for asking them to leave it on the flat-top griddle for a few more minutes.

I destroyed my burger with the fervour of a starving man, and then as we made our way back to our place I realized I was in serious trouble. I hadn't protested about the medium-rare burger but clearly I should have. I knew the feeling I was having; I was only minutes away from experiencing violent, bowl-splattering meat shits. Every red light was my enemy. I was squirming and shifting in my seat like a newborn baby who had filled his diaper. Lord, what I would have given to be wearing a diaper. I would have probably paid someone five thousand dollars that second for one Depends adult diaper sized extra-large men's. Sweat was pouring down my brow, and I was clutching and squeezing the steering wheel like I was wringing out a cloth.

"You okay?" asked Chobi.

"Oh, I'm fine, I'm fine," I replied, which both of us knew was a lie.

Pulling into our apartment building, I raced around the parking garage at a speed that alarmed my wife. She told me to slow down but the mission was simply too imminent. My insides were about to explode, and I needed to get on that toilet now.

Luckily for me, Chobi had decided to get off on the main floor and head to the 3rd Street Promenade a couple blocks away to do some shopping. At least I was going to have our apartment to myself. I wouldn't have to waste precious time stopping to turn on our stereo so my wife didn't hear me loudly shitting myself in our spare bathroom. (I always take my shits in the spare bathroom, mostly out of respect and also somewhat out of shame. It's humiliating how loud and disgusting I can be. Whenever we have guests at our place, which was very often during our first year in Los Angeles, it completely throws off my poop schedule.)

Chobi got off on the first floor and, unbelievably, a Chinese couple got on the elevator and hit "3," meaning my ascent was going to be stalled once again. What is it about being on an elevator that makes you have to poop *faster*? The Chinese couple stared at me with confused looks on their faces as I danced on the spot, shifting my feet back and forth and hopping up and down. We had reached a crisis point. My sphincter could only clench so much and was now being asked to do the impossible—that is, to hold back my waste for a few more precious seconds so I could sprint to my toilet. The couple got off on 3 and I tapped the "close door" button with the speed of my eight-year-old self hitting "fire" on a *Galaga* game. Was this elevator possibly going *slower*? We reached the fourth floor, then the fifth. *Can't . . . hold on . . . much longer.* I actually thought I might just break down and cry at that point.

Finally, like the gates to the Kingdom of Heaven, the doors opened on the top floor and I was just twenty steps from relief. I stepped briskly off the elevator and was shocked by what I saw in front of me.

The entire hallway was filled with furniture: stacks of chairs, a dresser, and several boxes piled up along the wall. The door to the apartment that had the eviction notices was propped open, and two Mexican guys walked out and looked at me. It was very clear what was going on here. The guy next door was getting out of there and skipping out on his rent. A scheduled move would have meant that Carl, our building supervisor, would have put protective padding up on the elevator to prevent any damage since our building had only the one elevator. Even in my sweaty, desperate state I knew that no such protective padding had been put up, which meant this was a covert operation. Our neighbour was skipping town.

The two Mexican guys and I stared at each other for a second, we nodded, and then I was jolted into the realization that I needed to get into my apartment *immediately.*

I turned away from the Mexican guys and stuck my hand in the front pocket of my jeans, fumbling for my keys, which I pulled out with a very shaky paw. The sweat was pouring down my forehead now, and as I attempted to stick my front door key into the keyhole I thought the opening may actually have shrunk right in front of my eyes, or maybe it was just my mind playing tricks on me. Either way I was having no luck whatsoever opening the door. It felt like one of those bad dreams where someone is chasing you to your front door and you desperately try to get it open while the pursuant gets closer and closer to you. Only this situation was slightly different. This was me struggling to get the key into the lock while I sweated desperately and my sphincter held on for dear life. I looked back toward my neighbour's door and saw the Mexicans continuing to stare at me, unsure whether they should help and probably confused over why I was sweating so profusely.

It was at that point that my body decided it couldn't take it anymore. I had pushed it to the limit. And with a sound that was remarkably similar to air being let out of a balloon, my sphincter gave out, and a trickle of shit sputtered out of my bum hole and down my leg as I continued to lock eyes with the Mexicans. Thankfully, this was an unusually cool spring day in Los Angeles and I was wearing a pair of Levi's and not the Gap shorts that were my usual off-work uniform. The Mexicans were spared the sight of my waste, but they could certainly hear it. Still, they showed no reaction. They just continued to stare straight at me as I fumbled with the door until finally, miraculously, the key went in and the door unlocked. I turned away from the Mexicans, threw the keys down on the floor and ran—*sprinted*—to the guest bathroom, where I tore off my belt and yanked down my pants faster than a fourteen-year-old invited to have sex for the first time. The relief I felt when I plopped down on that toilet seat was almost better than sex. Shit poured out of me like I was a container of freshly blended Jamba Juice: lumpy, clumpy, but soft and smooth as well. I had a gigantic, ridiculous grin on my face as I collapsed forward and ran my hands through my hair in a feeling of relief I hadn't experienced for quite some time. I was so desperately happy I hadn't completely crapped my pants in the hallway and even more delighted that my wife was not here to witness her disgusting husband deal with his weak and possibly damaged digestive system.

There was no need for toilet paper, as I would have been better served with a beach towel. Instead, I jumped directly into the shower to clean myself of any remaining bum residue and then threw the soiled jeans and undies directly into the washing machine. I took a paper towel and wiped down every surface in the bathroom using disinfectant spray. Chobi would never know about the massacre in our guest bathroom.

When she returned that afternoon with shopping bags in hand I was just waking up from a nap. That shit had taken a lot out of me both physically and emotionally, and my mind and body needed the rest. Chobi let me go back to sleep, and then an hour or so later, groggy and drowsy, I awakened and tried to embrace her only to be met with resistance and a scrunched-up frown on her face. "What's wrong?" I asked, barely coherent.

"Did you have a little accident in the bathroom?"

What the hell? How did she know? I had covered my tracks, literally. How did she know? *Had I married a witch?*

"Um, maybe. How could you have possibly known?"

"Because I walked in there to tidy up and I lifted up the toilet seat."

Oh, God. I had forgotten to check under the toilet seat.

"It looked like you were spackling drywall, or worse, it looked like you were Jackson Pollock in reverse."

My bowel movement had been so violent, so scattershot, that it had sprayed and splashed up and hit the bottom of the toilet seat and stuck there. It very likely hit my own ass as well, but my little sojourn in the shower took care of that foul residue. My tendency to hate the kind of guy who always forgets to put the toilet seat down—that guy who learned so little from his mother that he just walks out of the bathroom after pissing and never even thinks about it—my fear of being *that guy*, had instilled in me the need to leave the seat down every time I left the bathroom. One quick check could have prevented this, but now my wife would never be able to look at me the same way again after cleaning up my toilet spackle.

Just a day after I had promised my wife that I would never make a mess of myself in front of her like Chael Sonnen did in front of his wife, I had broken that promise in the worst way possible.

Chapter 17

The Sochi Sojourn, Part 1: Getting There

Fox did not have any rights whatsoever to broadcast the Sochi 2014 Winter Olympic Games. So why did Dan and I get to go to Russia? Because we *asked*. That's pretty much it. We *love* the Olympics, and we'd built up a lot of goodwill moving to Los Angeles, so when we heard that Fox was sending over a crew, we said we'd love to be a part of it. The next day we were told we were going. Very few people that we worked with understood our reasoning for wanting to go, especially to a small Russian city that by all accounts was having some significant troubles with preparation and accommodation. But these people hadn't been to the last two Olympics. I wanted to keep the streak going!

The timing wasn't exactly ideal as Fox had the rights to the Super Bowl that year, and to promote our show they'd put a giant billboard of Dan and me in Times Square in the hopes that we'd gain some momentum after Super Bowl week. Instead, once Super Bowl week was over we hightailed it across the pond. *Oops.*

We were never great with timing.

I took a cab with my wife to the Tom Bradley Terminal at the Los Angeles International Airport—it's the only thing keeping Angelenos from being completely embarrassed about living in a world-class city with the world's shittiest airport. The new terminal, completed in 2013, is a dazzler. It's filled with high-end stores—there's even a Fred Segal!—and celebrity chef Michael Voltaggio is opening a restaurant soon. Sea urchin foam before you take off to Barcelona for more sea urchin foam.

By comparison, whenever I drop Chobi off at Terminal 2, it seems like punishment now. Terminal 2 is the "Canadian" terminal, where we usually fly out when heading home, and I think it's deliberately shitty to encourage Canadians not to come back.

Dan and I flew out of Terminal 2 on our way to Calgary not long after we started at Fox. We were scheduled to host a golf tournament for Hockey Alberta in Canmore and lucky enough to be flying first class to the event. Wandering around the Air Canada lounge, which is more like some crappy bus station, we spotted *Batman Begins* and *Inception* director Christopher Nolan and his family. I wanted to apologize to him: "Please don't hold this terminal against our country, Christopher. I swear you're going to have a good time up in Rocky Mountain House or Medicine Hat or whatever small town you've selected as a stand-in for your apocalyptic vision of hell. I also promise not to be insulted that you've picked a part of my home province to stand in for hell."

After saying goodbye to Chobi, I walked the several hundred metres to the Tom Bradley Terminal and checked in to my Aeroflot flight. Not familiar with Aeroflot? Well, it's Russia's national airline, of course! Now I know what you're thinking: The stewardesses will all look like Bond girls and the main course in first class will be blinis and sour cream with a side of Russian vodka. But I'm here to tell you that . . . well, yeah, that's pretty much exactly how it was.

I have to confess, I went in a bit skeptical. Dan and I were allowed to fly direct to Moscow as a "reward" for all our hard work at Fox, while the rest of our crew had to make a stop in Frankfurt. But the Frankfurt stop meant the rest of the crew would be flying the much more established German airline, Lufthansa, while we took our chances with the Russians. I hadn't exactly heard great reviews, but like just about everything we encountered in Russia, they had polished things up just enough to get by.

As we were called to our flight, Dan noticed a famous Olympian would be travelling with us: Evan Lysacek, the American figure skater who shocked the world by beating Russian Evgeni Plushenko for the gold medal at Vancouver 2010. No longer skating, Lysacek was now commentating for NBC. I couldn't help but notice his impeccable Louis Vuitton carry-on luggage, complete with leather luggage tags that said "EL." *Time to step up my own luggage game*, I thought to myself.

We boarded the Aeroflot A330 Airbus, which for some reason was pungent with the rich smell of sulphur, and I was reminded of a time when I worked in a newsroom where one of my co-anchors ate a hard-boiled egg at their desk every single night. *Every. Single. Night.* Invariably, that colleague would sit directly behind me, and at some point in the night I would turn around and say, "Who farted?" only to see them sheepishly peeling away tiny bits of shell from the stinky treasure that awaited inside. When I left to take another job I almost missed that pungent odour.

The flight was better than expected once we were up in the air and free of the smell—maybe it was one of the bathrooms at LAX and not Vladimir Putin's farts powering this old but mighty winged monster. Immediately, I noticed a few quirks. The standard safety video wasn't standard at all. It featured 1980s community-cable-era effects and pounding techno so loud O'Toole and I couldn't even hear each other speak. Then there was the part of the safety video where we were instructed to turn off all electronic devices. At that point a picture of a boom box appeared on the screen. A *boom box*.

Twelve hours later we arrived in Moscow and were greeted by a smiling group of Russian teenagers with colourful Sochi 2014 jackets made by the official supplier to the host country's Olympic team: Bosco. That's right, the Nike of Russia was named after the pin code for George Costanza's ATM card on *Seinfeld* . . . probably.

Dan was still a little sore about the fact that his in-flight TV hadn't worked and his seat wouldn't recline, but he started beaming at the sight of these friendly volunteers. Little did I know this wonderful group of kids would serve as a precursor to the treatment we would receive from *all* the volunteers at the Sochi Games. One of them removed a sticker from a sheet in his hand and placed it firmly on my arm like I was a box of tampons in the local pharmacy. The other volunteers found him hilarious and that—combined with his diminutive stature—led me to dub him "Russia's Aziz Ansari," which I assume he found funny, though he claimed not to know who that was. Russian Aziz laughed and smiled and said: "Welcome to Sochi! Follow me!" and we did. Dan, me, Lysacek, and the whole weary, groggy gang followed these Russian teenagers straight through the international terminal of the Moscow airport, prompting Lysacek to wonder why we hadn't been tied to a long rope like a bunch of kindergarten students.

Onward we walked past the Irish pub serving quesadillas and the cafés with pies filled with "meat and cheese" to our next gate and a smaller plane that would take us to Sochi. Immediately, I felt transported back to the early '80s—the entire terminal stunk of cigarette smoke. Of course, no one was actually allowed to smoke in the terminal, but that didn't stop everyone from crowding into the airport bathrooms like a bunch of school kids in *Dazed and Confused*. In Russia, we soon learned, people smoke *everywhere*. Bars, restaurants, schools, you name it and Russians were still smoking there—*a lot*. It was kind of neat actually. I say "neat" because I realize smoking kills thousands of people every year and it's a terrible habit, but as someone who still remembers coming home from the bar at night stinking of DuMaurier Lights, I have to admit I felt a bit nostalgic. And I've never even smoked!

When we finally arrived at the Sochi airport after two flights that totaled fourteen hours, I was met with another shock. We'd heard reports from colleagues who'd arrived early about brown water in hotel bathrooms and stray dogs wandering into rooms ("I hope there's a puppy in my room!" I tweeted), so when we stepped off the airplane into a thoroughly modern and spectacularly clean airport, I was pleasantly surprised. The airport had obviously been renovated for the Games, but I was still impressed by the effort of the Russians to make a good first impression.

Dan and I were greeted by Jorge Mondaca, a Fox production assistant who had spent much of the past year preparing for our coverage of the Sochi Games. At a meeting with Jorge and the senior executive on the project, Rick Jaffe, a month before we'd been presented with a two-inch-thick binder filled with information that would help us prepare for our coverage: day-by-day breakdowns of events and the names of the Americans who were likely to medal in them; a detailed description of what was expected of us by Fox with regard to coverage; security information and emergency contacts; and even restaurant and bar recommendations. You'll likely remember what I've always said was the motto of Canadian television: "We'll figure it out when we get there." Well, it turns out the motto of American television is "We'll figure it out before we leave, and we'll also tell you where to get a decent cappuccino."

Jorge had been driven to the airport by Igor, one of our three drivers for the trip. Igor spoke exactly zero English and was built like a Stampede Wrestling–era version of the Dynamite Kid. But he was also pleasant and smiled a lot, and he took half our bags and led us out the front door of the terminal. Jorge insisted on taking the rest of the bags, despite our protests, and so we stepped out onto the pavement and caught our first whiff of Russian air. Not bad. Even better was the appearance of our first Sochi stray dog.

Much had been made leading up to the Games about the prevalence of Sochi strays around the Olympic Park and the fate that may have befallen them—stories of flatbed trucks sweeping the back alleyways and picking them up like the puppies in *101 Dalmatians*, then transporting them to an untimely and horrifying death. We'd also heard stories of mysterious Russian billionaires rescuing said dogs and taking them to a beautiful sanctuary in the hills surrounding St. Petersburg, where they could run and jump and play and live happy lives shepherded by a fat old woman named Dashinka. I'm not exactly sure where the truth lay, but that first dog we saw coming out of the airport seemed neither sad nor underfed. Rather, he was pleasantly friendly, healthy, and jittery, in need of nothing more than a long, soapy bath. Maybe he was the airport dog?

We climbed into one of two Audi Q7s that Fox had rented for our transportation in and around Sochi. We wouldn't come into contact with the third vehicle until the next day, and that was probably a good thing because after fourteen hours in the air, the sight of the Street Dragon might have been too much for us to handle. More on that to come.

The drive through Sochi to our hotel wasn't a drive through Sochi at all, but rather a drive through Adler, a town adjacent to Sochi where the Olympic Park was located. After twisting through several backstreets, past twenty-four-hour liquor stores and concrete block houses that had seen better days, we arrived at our destination, La Terrassa.

La Terrassa describes itself as a "boutique" hotel. I guess that could be true if by boutique hotel you meant a cross between a two-star hotel and a Victorian frat house. Let me get this out of the way: Compared with the hotels of some of our colleagues visiting Sochi, our accommodations were more than adequate. We made our way into the lobby area and I was immediately—and pleasantly—surprised by the surroundings: marble floors, a *real* bar, and what looked to be comfortable chairs. I was given a key to my room, and when I got upstairs I was even more impressed. I'd been given a reasonably large suite, complete with a couch, chairs, and what's this? A kitchenette? Nope . . . false alarm. That kitchen wasn't quite finished. The water wasn't hooked up. The sink wasn't installed. So, someone decided to just turn it into a closet and call it a day.

Weary from my travels, I decided to just sit down and . . . the back of the chair collapsed and I fell on my ass. I guess they didn't have time to make real chairs either.

Still, the bed was comfortable enough and the shower pressure was decent. What's more, there was no dog in my room, and no (visible) semen stains on the bed. This was going to be okay! I went back downstairs to collect my bags from the lobby.

Jorge was there to greet me.

"How's the room?" he asked.

"Really nice, actually! Thanks so much. Where're my bags?"

"Here it is," said Jorge, as he handed me a small piece of carry-on luggage.

"Where's the other bag?" I asked.

"What other bag?" he replied, looking puzzled.

"The other bag that I brought with me from Los Angeles. The big suitcase? The one you said I should let you carry out of the airport?"

"Oh, no . . . Igor!" he said. *Sure.* Blame the guy who can't defend himself in English.

It turns out my other bag was sitting right next to that healthy looking stray dog by the front doors of the Sochi airport. Somehow Jorge had assumed Igor was picking it up, or perhaps Igor had assumed Jorge was picking it up. Either way, I vowed to start carrying my own bags from then on while I pondered a wardrobe of brightly coloured Bosco Olympic shirts and perhaps a Cossack uniform if I could get the hotel to rent one for me. Igor sped back to the airport with Jorge and they found my bag sitting right where he . . . they . . . me . . . *someone* had left it. That Sochi stray dog was sniffing around it and had probably marked it several times. Was this a bad sign?

Chapter 18

The Sochi Sojourn, Part 2: Olympic Life

On our first full day in Russia, we woke up late after consuming one too many draft beers at the lobby bar of our hotel, La Terrassa. A young man named Artem had been serving them up for us. He didn't speak English, so we began communicating using the power of Google Translate, which I am convinced would have prevented most wars had it been introduced centuries ago. The thrill of typing in English and having it magically appear in Russian, then handing it over to Artem, who instantly smiled in recognition, was a feeling of joy and relief I hadn't experienced in some time. Technology is truly wonderful! I mean, how else would I get my beer on? And in addition to pulling a mean pint, Artem and the other guys behind the bar could whip up a pretty mean cappuccino too. We're talking Seattle indie coffeehouse quality here.

Visiting the Olympic Park for the first time, I was impressed with what the Russians had accomplished. The entire concept was very clear: Keep all the venues as close as possible. The Olympic Park had been built on a plot of land that was basically abandoned before the Olympics, giving the organizers a chance to put everything within walking distance.

Our first stop that day was Canada Olympic House—a building where the athletes and their families could gather and enjoy drinks and food and familiar Canadian treats like Caramilk Bars and ketchup chips, all in a comfortable setting. It was also home to the offices for the Canadian Olympic Committee and a small store where you could purchase official merchandise. Unlike London, where the various Olympic houses were scattered all over that massive city, in Sochi almost all the houses were inside the Olympic Park itself. The lone exception was Holland House, fully sponsored by Heineken and as usual the biggest party in town. They decided to set up shop behind one of the bigger (and nicer) hotels so they could stay open later and have a bit more real estate. It was a brilliant concept. The Dutch national broadcaster, Olympic House, and the athletes' lounge were all part of the same complex, so when someone like star speed skater Sven Kramer won a medal they could interview him and get him drunk in one comfortable setting.

Perhaps it was a coincidence, but Canada Olympic House and USA Olympic House were situated right beside each other. The Canadian house was a two-story affair and towered over the more austere, bungalow-like USA House, and the differences carried over inside. Soon after we arrived I went with U.S. Olympic figure skater Michelle Kwan, who'd been hired by Fox to work as a commentator during the Games, to learn about the U.S. bobsled team's new sled, designed by BMW. The coaches of the men's and women's teams gave us a bit of instruction, and then we sardined ourselves into the sled. Poor Michelle probably wished she had never agreed to the exercise. Luckily, we were on dry land or we probably would have both been seriously injured. After the demo we wandered around the restaurant/lounge area and I commented on how quiet and buttoned up things seemed to be. Even when the place was packed, as it was when we stopped by with another newly hired Fox commentator a few days later—former U.S. Olympic hockey player and NHL Hall of Famer Chris Chelios—it still had the air of a quiet afternoon dinner party at the Barefoot Contessa's house.

Meanwhile, next door at Canada House, the decidedly cozier confines on the main floor gave the place a more raucous party atmosphere, like a small pub in Ontario cottage country but with slightly better furniture and Canadian Olympians wandering around. In a way we felt a bit conflicted about being there—like we were taking advantage of the situation. We had no reason or right to walk through the door, if I'm being honest. We were broadcasting for an American audience who on the whole probably had very little idea who Tessa Virtue or Scott Moir was. We felt a little sheepish when we'd wander up to the place, walk in, and ask for a few guest passes so we could show some of our friends from Fox what Canadian hospitality was all about.

The first time we stopped by Canada Olympic House the Russian security guard outside eyed me up like I was coming to return Bieber to the Canadians. He looked like a younger Jean Reno, but after our initial, somewhat tension-filled first meeting, he seemed to warm up to me. Suddenly, I was breezing right past him on my way to the front desk, where I was likely bringing in more Americans to see the place and enjoy a free pint of Miller Genuine Draft. (The Molson Canadian, much like our Fox Olympic winter jackets, had been "held up" at customs. That's not a joke. Fox had ordered about fifty beautiful winter jackets for our entire crew, and one of our senior executives spent much of the first week negotiating with customs to get them back. The price continued to go up and up until he abandoned the idea of retrieving them altogether.)

One thing that was *not* held up in customs was the Molson Canadian beer fridge, a genius bit of marketing by the Molson Coors group. A beer fridge was placed at the back of the Canada Olympic House near the bar, and the only way to open it was by using your Canadian passport, which you carefully slid into a slot in the front. You would hear a "click" and presto! Free beer!

We brought along one of our web producers to demonstrate that a U.S. passport would not work while we gleefully cracked the fridge with our Canadian credentials. The Molson Canadian PR staff on site were delighted that we stopped by, and they retweeted the web video we put together about the fridge. We decided to invite the Molson PR staff back to La Terrassa later that evening for some drinks and socializing and perhaps a few leftover breakfast potatoes from the morning buffet. Like everyone who stopped by "the Frat House," we led the team around our hotel for a tour, which included climbing all five flights to the top floor where we shot our segments for *Fox Sports Live* every night.

Leaning over the balcony as we admired the Olympic Park across the street that night, I couldn't help but notice what might best be described as a "commotion" about a block away directly in front of an apartment building where several of our staff had been put up during the Games—including our three Russian makeup artists. A massive crowd had gathered and an ambulance was on the scene.

"That doesn't look good," said Tonia, one of the Molson PR staff, who was just about to celebrate her birthday and probably wished she was anywhere else but this bizarre Russian hotel at the moment.

Indeed, it did not look good at all. An ambulance called in around one in the morning in the middle of Adler could not mean good things. We went back to the lobby to get the Molson girls some drinks. Our new friend, Fox NFL reporter turned Fox figure skating reporter Peter Schrager, kept saying to anyone who would listen that there was a serious situation happening just down the street and perhaps we should be concerned about it—or at least for the safety of *our* crew. From our vantage point, it seemed like there was a serious discussion happening among the Fox Network heavy hitters who were running the show on our end, but no immediate danger. *Must have been a heart attack or something like that*, I thought to myself, and gave it little more thought as the nighttime turned into daytime once again on our Sochi sojourn.

Even though I had shut things down at the usual time—around five in the morning—I found myself unable to sleep at 9:00 a.m. and decided to join the gang that went over to the gym and spa at the nearby Radisson Blu Hotel, which we were allowed access to thanks to a couple of our senior Fox production people. I threw on a T-shirt and jeans, chucked a pair of swim trunks into my official Sochi 2014 backpack, provided compliments of the local organizing committee, and plodded downstairs to the lobby to see who was waiting for Kostya, our driver and all-around great guy. One of Artem's cappuccinos steadied my nerves a bit, and I noticed our Russia-based producers (I made the mistake of introducing them as our "translators" once and they didn't speak to me for two days), Irina and Dasha, sitting in the lobby looking unusually forlorn. I skipped over to them.

"Good morning, ladies," I said with a grin. My full smile was not yet returned.

"Morning," said Irina flatly.

"What's wrong? What's going on?" I asked.

She looked around, then stared straight into my eyes.

"A woman died last night."

"Huh?"

"Crowd outside the apartment down the street. Last night. They were surrounding woman who fell off balcony and died."

What a shocking bit of news to get on just four hours of barely sober sleep.

Hours later, the entire staff, almost forty of us, was summoned to the fourth-floor studios for a debriefing, henceforth known somewhat insensitively as "the Murder Meeting." Jeff Husvar, a Fox executive VP, who was running the operation, struck a sombre tone as he explained the situation. It turned out the apartment across from the one Fox was using for its employees was being rented out to several migrant workers who were responsible for building and maintaining the Olympic venues. The apartments in the building were intended for a family of four but were likely housing as many as twenty-five men—*each*—throughout the course of the Games. On the previous night, three men were outside on the top-floor balcony when an argument broke out. A woman intervened to break up the argument and somehow *accidentally* tumbled over the edge of the balcony to her death.

Uh huh.

Regardless of what we thought about the story, this was the company line and little could be done about it now. The main concern going forward was obviously security. A woman had fallen to her death under suspicious circumstances directly across the street from our accommodation. It was determined that no one staying in those apartments would be allowed to walk back and forth to the studios at La Terrassa without being accompanied by one of our security team, who were usually just hanging around the lobby and would likely welcome the opportunity to go for a little walk anyway. After the meeting was over I returned to the lobby to sit down and speak with Robert Lusetich, our Fox *golf* reporter and columnist who was given the *snowboarding* beat in Sochi. (I'll pause to allow you to read that sentence again.) Robert and I were discussing the events of the previous evening, when Natasha, one of our beautiful Russian makeup artists, sauntered through the door all by herself. Not a single person accompanied her on her walk from the apartment—the same apartment where a woman fell to her death not twenty-four hours prior.

"New plan is working pretty well," said Robert.

Partway through our stay in Sochi, we decided to take a trip up to Rosa Khutor Mountain Village to see if we could find some interesting material for a story. Predictably, after getting dropped off, our first stop was the McDonald's for a little sustenance. I should mention that over the course of my fourteen or so days in Sochi I ate at McDonald's approximately fifteen times. I hated becoming one of those Western tourists who didn't bother trying the local cuisine because it was foreign to them. That wasn't the reason we made the trek to McD's every day. The real reason was that La Terrassa was beginning to resemble a really bad all-inclusive resort, and we couldn't handle the smell coming out of the kitchen anymore. The first day or so we were pleasantly surprised: "This food isn't bad!" But then we realized the exact same food would be placed in front of us every single day like we were at a medium-security prison. Once the cook in the kitchen had determined a few mostly Western dishes seemed to be popular with our group, she just kept cranking out those same dishes over and over again, rather than serving up something she was probably more familiar with preparing. The food at the restaurants around Sochi wasn't much better. So McDonald's became a daily staple. Between the Big Macs and the vodka, Dan and I returned from Russia carrying approximately fifty extra pounds.

Each.

Back in the mountain cluster, we wandered around the mile-long stretch of hotels, restaurants, and shops that was finished, oh, about six or seven minutes before we showed up. The whole place was really beautiful but still had the distinct look and feel of a theme-park version of a mountain ski village. All I could think the whole time we were there was *Who will come here to ski?* North Americans? It's unlikely that the ones with enough scratch to put together a transcontinental ski trip would make it past the Alps. It's not as if you could fly directly into Sochi or anything. The whole venture just didn't seem like it was worth the trouble. Native Russians? Maybe, but how many of them had the money to make the trek down to Sochi? The ones I talked to wanted to go to New York or the Caribbean, not spend their hard-earned holiday dollars on a ski trip in their own backyard. The question came up again and again everywhere we went in Sochi: What would this place look like in ten years? The problem was no one seemed willing to come back here in ten years' time to find out.

After unsuccessfully trying to put together some sort of "story" in which Dan and I checked out an open-air cafeteria where you were served by Cossacks and Russian women in peasant skirts and headdresses, we abandoned the idea of accomplishing anything constructive and made our way to the Rosa Khutor Extreme Park, a place I could not say the name of without either bursting into laughter or coming up with my own theme song for the place:

DON'T GO OUT ON A LARK ...

JUST HIT THE ROSA KHUTOR EXTREME PARK!

The lyrics were rudimentary but the sentiment was there.

We met up with Chris Chelios and Andy Finch at the halfpipe event. Andy was a professional snowboarder who competed in the first ever Olympic halfpipe in Turin, Italy, back in 2006. He was the epitome of a surfer dude who grew up in California and spoke in a long, slow drawl. He was a wonderful guy, partial to wearing flip-flops everywhere, and at one point during the Games decided to complete the trifecta of snowboarding, surfing, and skateboarding in the same day—all of which he was able to capture on tape via a GoPro camera attached to his helmet. He also amazed us on the final day of the Games when he retired to his hotel room and came back with a violin, which he proceeded to play for us *by ear*. Any song we would play on our laptops Andy would listen to for a second and then play note for note right in front of us—the result of lessons taken from age six to eighteen. Quite a party trick. He and Chelios bonded early in the Games, sort of an opposites-attract-via-mutual-respect type of thing. Chelly was a Malibu resident who had become good friends with big-wave surfer Laird Hamilton, and he and Andy got along great. Andy would quietly explain the minute details of snowboarding to Chris, and then when we attended Olympic hockey games I'd hear Chris explaining line changes and power plays to Andy.

At the Rosa Khutor Extreme Park that afternoon we watched Shawn White put together a flawless qualifying run in the Olympic slopestyle event. Sitting in the stands at the bottom of the run was a tremendously rewarding experience. Throughout the other riders' runs music blared from the speakers—hip hop, pop, rock—while images of the riders flashed on a giant screen at the top of the hill. The whole thing felt more like an event at the X Games world tour than the Olympics. When White took his turn, though, the entire mountain seemed to fall silent. No music played, no one made a sound—it was almost like the whole world stood still for a minute and a half so we could all bask in the greatness of this world-class athlete. And he *was* world class, soaring higher than any of the other riders by a long shot. All the riders were talented and capable athletes, but what separated Shawn White from the pack was the incredible air he got on his jumps—it was almost superhuman. And when he reached the bottom of the mountain to rumbling applause and enthusiastic foot-stomping from Andy, it seemed that nothing could possibly keep this man from a third consecutive gold medal.

Alas, when White went for the gold later that evening, he proved he was indeed human, hitting the lip of the ramp on both of his medal runs and falling off the podium altogether. It was a great example of why I could never have become an Olympic athlete. Even if I had the necessary ability, I could never wrap my head around the idea of training four years for one single day of competition where a single slip-up could cost you a medal—even if, like Shawn White, I was clearly the best athlete competing that day. I couldn't reconcile all that work with a failed result. I wouldn't be able to live with myself.

No one understood this better than Michelle Kwan, who had won the World Figure Skating Championships nine consecutive times but fallen short twice in Olympic competition. After witnessing Canadian Patrick Chan fail to take advantage of a fall from Japanese skater Yuzuru Hanyu and finish a disappointing second in the men's singles, Michelle commented that she really wanted to speak with Patrick about the competition because he hadn't fully experienced the shattering disappointment that was to come. She mentioned that she had suffered through nightmares following her Olympic competition. The pure fact of the matter was that Michelle had handled the crushing disappointment with as much grace and class as any single human being could ever be expected to. She seemed at least outwardly to have moved on with her life, and if walking into the Iceberg Skating Palace alongside Michelle was any proof, she was certainly well loved by the international skating community. *Worshipped* is more like it. "Like walking into a castle with the queen," Schrager said.

It was nice to spend the afternoon hanging with Chelios and Finch and Dan. We enjoyed perhaps our best meal in Russia up to that point: "Brooklyn" hotdogs. At the Sochi Games, that meant a hotdog smothered in what could best be described as Cheez Whiz, with just slightly undercooked bacon pieces sprinkled over top. After a week of meals at La Terrassa, that "Brooklyn" hotdog was like foie gras on a ribeye for a carnivore like me. Afterwards, we hopped in the media shuttle—essentially a school bus—and made our way back down to the Rosa Khutor Mountain Village where we were scheduled to meet Vlad in the Street Dragon.

For me, the Street Dragon became one of the most enduring symbols of the 2014 Olympic Winter Games. The Audi Q7s were obviously beautiful, solid, dependable vehicles, but the Street Dragon was kind of like their opposite. If I were to estimate, I'd say the Street Dragon was a mid-'90s Toyota minivan that had mysteriously been stripped of the handle on the sliding door. And the Street Dragon wasn't just a tongue-in-cheek name given to the vehicle by Schrager; it was actually *written* on the side in the form of a decal that included an elaborate tattoo-style dragon. The decal was black, the van was white, and the driver spoke not a single word of English. Often when driving with Vlad in the Street Dragon he would change the song on his MP3 player (no door handle, but the latest in audio technology) while simultaneously taking part in a spirited discussion on his iPhone. One person on the trip informed me that during a ride he asked Vlad the password for the van's Wi-Fi hotspot. (Yes, the van had Wi-Fi—again, technology one might want to set up *after* fixing the door handle.) Vlad then proceeded to reach back and take the person's phone to punch in the Wi-Fi password as he controlled the wheel with his knees. With all this in mind, we saw Vlad at the curb as the media shuttle dropped us off at the Mountain Village. Chris, Dan, and Andy climbed into the back of the Street Dragon, and I hopped in the front. Little did I know I was about to endure the most terrifying ride of my life.

During the half-hour ride back to La Terrassa I saw my life flash in front of my eyes at least six times. That's the exact number of times Vlad pulled into the left lane to pass and I saw another vehicle careening toward us at maximum speed with no apparent regard for the impending doom they were heading straight for. Each and every time, at the very last second, Vlad would pull us back safely into the right lane, all the while maintaining his own breakneck speed. It was as if Liam Neeson from *Taken* were piloting the vehicle with his very particular set of skills, and he had only a finite amount of time to get back to this rather suspect "boutique" hotel to save his wife and daughter. Vlad had a particular set of skills all right—the ability to log on to Wi-Fi while barrelling down a highway on the edge of the Red Sea at a God-forsaken pace; the ability to not understand any English except when someone asked him about Wi-Fi passwords; and the ability to select pretty darn cool tunes for the Street Dragon—and I mean that sincerely (I will never again be able to hear "Bahama Mama" by Boney M without thinking of Vlad and the Street Dragon).

With each close call I got more and more excited. Vlad was a man who clearly understood the streets of rural Russia. Would I want my loved ones to travel with this guy? Hell, no. But the truth is the drive back to Adler from Rosa Khutor Mountain Village was more exciting than any ride at Disneyland. I began to encourage Vlad, daring him to take more chances and pass more slow-moving vehicles. All the while the peanut gallery in the back were trying to ruin my fun, shouting about concepts like "safety" and "massive four-car accidents" and "lawsuits." The only thing that slowed Vlad down was finally getting off the freeway into the urban landscape of downtown Adler. But even then Vlad wasn't out for a Sunday drive. Running up against the bumpers of cars and trucks in front of us and liberally using his horn, pushing the speed limits all the while. The whole thing really made me laugh, but I was clearly in the minority. Everyone else in the vehicle had already made the silent decision to never enter the Street Dragon again.

When we finally pulled past the security gate at La Terrassa and the sliding door was opened (from the inside of course), Chris Chelios was the first to spill out. He calmly walked over to the driver's side door where Vlad was sitting, smiling and waiting for us to get out so he could be told about the next person he was scheduled to pick up and terrify. Chris looked him straight in the eye and said: "SLOW. DOWN."

Vlad just kept on smiling.

Chapter 19

The Sochi Sojourn, Part 3: Gold-Medal Hockey

As members of the press at Sochi 2014, Dan and I had little difficulty getting into events. Typically, just our Olympic credentials were enough to get us past security. But for some high-demand events, we needed our credentials *and* a ticket. And tickets to the big events were scarce. If Fox had any, they always went to the reporters actually covering the event—and like those infamous Sochi strays, Dan and I fed off the scraps.

Take figure skating, for example. Our two designated Fox tickets went to the people actually covering the events, Peter Schrager and our figure skating analyst, Michelle Kwan. But after the first night of competition, they returned to La Terrassa and reported that the security team at the Iceberg Skating Palace was not actually *checking* the tickets for authenticity, barely lifting their heads when Michelle and Peter flashed them. So I ended up sneaking into the Iceberg a few times by taking Michelle's ticket from the previous evening and strategically placing my finger or thumb over the date. Each and every time I attempted the move, I breezed by the crack security team like I was a ghost. I probably should have been more alarmed by how easy it was for me to sneak into a secured Olympic venue, but I was just too thrilled to worry about it.

And thanks to this scam, I was there to see Evgeni Plushenko make his final appearance in front of an adoring home crowd. Unfortunately, that meant witnessing him struggle through the warm-up, then skate over to the judges and pull out of the competition, subsequently retiring from the sport a few hours later. I hadn't seen the life sucked out of a room that fast since our inebriated London makeup artist collapsed in front of 300 Canadians at a closing ceremonies party.

The gold-medal hockey game in Sochi didn't have quite the same buildup and cache as the one in Vancouver—and rightly so. Not only was host nation Russia eliminated before the semifinals, but they had bowed out in a rather depressing fashion. The Games had started well enough for the Russians with a 5-2 win over Slovenia and then a very exciting shootout loss to the United States—that game had one of the best atmospheres I've experienced in my life. The Bolshoy Ice Dome held just under 13,000 spectators, so it was significantly smaller than the arena for the 2010 Games in Vancouver. But the place was absolutely rammed with Russians, and it was a treat to stand beside them as they rode the roller coaster of emotion during the shootout, eventually falling to heartbreak when T.J. Oshie beat my old friend Sergei Bobrovsky for the winning goal.

So much was made of the fact that Alexander Ovechkin had planned to compete for Russia at the Sochi Games, regardless of whether or not the NHL gave its approval. And when the NHL finally *did* give its players the green light, the Russians became the early favourites based on home ice advantage, national pride, and an incredible wealth of hockey talent. Alas, like many Russian teams of the past, the 2014 roster just didn't play as a team. Ovechkin seemed practically invisible, which was truly unfortunate since his gap-toothed grin was plastered around the park and all over Sochi on Coca-Cola ads.

A few days after Team Russia was eliminated, Ovechkin's father suffered a heart attack. Thankfully, he survived. Still, I couldn't help but think how different the Games must have been from the way Ovechkin had envisioned them.

The other factor contributing to the lack of hype leading up to the gold-medal game was the matchup. Team Canada was playing better and better as the tournament went on, pouring 57 shots on Latvian goaltender Kristers Gudlevskis in the quarter-finals and then dispatching the U.S. in the semis. Really, the only surprise was the lacklustre, uninspired play of the Americans in that semifinal game against Canada. While down 1-0 in the third period, a "guaranteed to tie" situation if there ever was one, the U.S. basically stopped playing (or perhaps the Canadians wouldn't *let* them play). The end result was never really in doubt, and the Canadians breezed into the final to face the Swedes—a formidable opponent to be sure, but perhaps not the sexiest matchup for a North American or Russian hockey audience. Still, as a hockey fan I was aware Sweden was no pushover, especially with "King Henrik" Lundqvist between the pipes for the Tre Kroner.

As anyone familiar with *Anchorboy* will remember, I ran a marathon to get into the gold-medal game in 2010. Surely I could figure out a way to sneak into this one too. I mean, I couldn't come all the way to Russia and *not* go to the gold-medal game, could I?

Peter Schrager, being the crafty and charming man that he is, found a hookup for tickets. A friend at Nike had informed him that because of the Russian team's epic collapse earlier that week, a few tickets that had been earmarked for important clients within the country had suddenly become available. Schrags secured a pair of tickets soon after the semifinals, and then on the day of the game, he was promised an additional pair that he offered up to Dan and me. What a gem.

The only catch was that we would have to meet the Nike representative in possession of the tickets over at USA Olympic House before the game. *No problem*, I thought to myself. *This'll be a lot easier than running a marathon through the streets of Vancouver.*

I left Dan to sleep in at the hotel while I made my way over to the park to meet up with the Nike rep—I figured I'd meet up with Dan later before the game. Leaving La Terrassa for what was likely the last time, I headed down the sidewalk, past Mooka, the lazy but adorable dog who parked himself in front of the hotel; past the silent, sullen security guards who loitered around the gate without a word; and past the open sewer, with its rich, pungent-smelling contents—the remnants of the past few weeks in Sochi. I was going to . . . miss this place?

The truth is I *was* going to miss it, but not for the architecture or the questionable food or the occasional phantom odour that assaulted my nose. I would miss Sochi because of the people.

The Russian people were not at all like I had expected. It's such a cliché, but I seriously thought our entire time in Russia would be spent encountering cold, closed-off, sullen ex-Soviets forced to endure two weeks of hell with foreigners who didn't understand or appreciate them or their culture. Instead, I found everyone I met to be kind, warm, friendly, and completely supportive of my feeble attempts to speak their language. Everyone was extremely passionate about *being* Russian. At every venue the crowds were deafening for Russian athletes who happened to be competing. Regardless of the sport or gender of the athlete, if they saw that white stripe on top, that blue stripe in the middle, and that red stripe on the bottom, they were going to support their athletes and support them loudly. I didn't get into politics with the Russians much, but anytime a botoxed Vladmir Putin appeared on-screen I would look back at our driver, Kostya, and he would simply say, "Bullshit." A few weeks after we left Russia, the army was deployed along the border with Ukraine to "protect the safety and security of Russia." Safely back home in Los Angeles I wondered about Kostya and Dasha and Irina and all the young Russians we had encountered in Sochi. What did they think of this madness?

I continued to walk the streets of Sochi, through the initial security gate, through a second security gate, and past the International Broadcast Centre, which housed the McDonald's we'd eaten at so many times. Oh, how I would miss that McDonald's! I can remember vividly as a kid, in about the fifth or sixth grade, when the first ever "Russian" McDonald's opened up in Moscow's Red Square. It was international news. The lineups were said to be unfathomable. And now here I was, some thirty years later, attending and covering the Olympic Games in the same country, forever grateful that I had this familiar taste of home to enjoy almost every single day— health be damned. Finally, after walking another kilometre or so, I arrived at the last security gate before the Bolshoy Ice Dome, at which point I was stopped dead in my tracks by one of those nice friendly Russians.

"You need ticket," said the superkind and sweet female volunteer at the gate.

"My ticket is inside," I replied innocently.

"Sorry, you need ticket here," she said.

"I need a ticket here? I haven't needed a ticket here before."

"You need ticket here today," she said, with an air of finality.

Turns out that on this, the final day of the Sochi 2014 Olympic Winter Games, the Russians had decided to ramp up security and not let *anyone* into the park who wasn't carrying a ticket to the gold-medal hockey game or closing ceremonies. This was going to be a major problem. I had a ticket to the gold-medal hockey game for the second Olympics in a row, and for the second Olympics in a row I was faced with an obstacle that would push me to my physical limits, the physical limits of an inactive third grader. This was going to require some serious effort on my part.

I texted the number of Peter Schrager's Nike contact. She informed me she was running late and that she was on her way to USA Olympic House but would probably be ten or twenty minutes behind the originally scheduled time. At least this would give me some time to figure out how I might get into what was perhaps the most heavily secured one-mile radius in the world, next to the Vatican of course. I knew from experience that at the very least I could wander over to the Iceberg Skating Palace and see the people walking by inside the park through the chain link fence and over the barriers. Perhaps I could convince one of the guards to allow me to accept my ticket—*our* tickets—through the gate. There had to be a way. I just couldn't accept the idea of having a ticket to the second straight Olympic gold-medal game—a game taking place just over a kilometre away—and not actually getting to attend because I wasn't smart enough to figure out a way in. I would not allow this to happen. Not on my watch!

I ran from the "security gate of denial" about 500 metres to the Iceberg Skating Palace, where much to my surprise the media gate was accessible without any pass whatsoever. In fact, I strolled right up to the entrance of the Iceberg Skating Palace and was initially elated that I would be able to enter the park from there, only to realize that the reason they had allowed access to the facility was because it was completely empty. The entrance to the actual park had indeed been closed off. Not using any sophisticated means, mind you; there was no massive gate with barbed wire. Workers had simply taken two good-sized barricades and instead of standing them on their legs—like the original designer had intended— they had stacked them vertically and then crossed them over each other like giants might build a shoddy house of cards. This was the elaborate security system that had been set up on the side of the park where events were no longer taking place. Did I still feel comfortable about our safety in this part of the world? Had Russian promises about security been fulfilled? And more importantly, could I actually sneak into the 2014 Olympic Winter Games by hopping over a couple of barricades that were haphazardly leaned against each other like popsicle sticks?

I approached the "leaners" and looked around. Technically, I was already in the park, but the barricades were there to prevent me or anyone else from going any farther. Occasionally I would spot a security guy lurking outside the craft services building next door. The guy would usually give me a disinterested look and then turn away. This happened two or three times, as if he was saying, "I know you're probably up to no good, and I should do something about it, but I've been standing here for the past three weeks and you're clearly not a threat, so do what you need to do. I'll be over here waiting for you to go home."

It was entirely plausible that this might work, that I might be able to break into the park and meet the nice Nike lady with our tickets, and Dan and I would be able to watch Canada battle Sweden for a gold medal and everything would be all right! It would be just like when I had to run through the streets of Vancouver to fetch a ticket that had been promised to me for the gold-medal game in 2010. I would make it through all the obstacles before me now, just as I had then. Only this time, the obstacles were actual physical obstacles.

It was also entirely plausible that I might be caught by security and told to leave the country, never to return. Or that I might be caught by security and thrown into a Russian jail. So many fun possibilities.

When I was confident the security guy wasn't looking I made my move. Ten minutes had passed by this point, meaning that if the nice Nike lady was actually on time, I had only ten more minutes to make it to the rendezvous point. There was really no time to spare.

I thought of it like a ladder. I just had to carefully scale the barricades and climb over without the security guy seeing what I was doing. Simple. I put my size thirteen Nike into the first bar of the barricade, turned around, and there was the security guy. I felt a wave of panic go through me. But he simply smiled and shook his head, "no," then walked back to the craft services building.

I had come very close to shitting myself. As many of you know, I've shit myself in much less stressful situations in the past. Honestly, it's amazing I was able to maintain my constitution.

That very second, my phone rang. Thank God for the international data plan.

I reached into my back pocket, grabbed my phone, and answered it.

"Hello?"

"Jay? This is Irena from Nike!"

Oh, no.

"I'm still running a little late."

Yes!

"I'm so sorry for the inconvenience."

Little did she know she was actually saving my ass! Finally, I was catching a break.

"I'm actually having a little problem getting to the meeting point myself," I told her.

"Oh, yeah? Is the USA House not convenient for you?"

You might say that.

"I'm just having a little trouble getting past security today."

"Oh, yes, you need a ticket."

Thaaanks.

"Yeah, I know that now. Is there any chance we might be able to meet up somewhere outside of the park?"

"Sure, I have to meet my co-worker at the USA House. Perhaps I could meet you at the media entrance for the Adler speed skating arena?"

Yes! The media entrance was *outside* the security gate. I knew this from the countless times I had been back and forth to watch speed skating because of my lack of actual responsibilities during the day. This might actually work out for the best!

"I'll be right there!" I said.

"See you in a few minutes."

I hung up and saw that I had received a text from Dan. "Where are you we need tickets to get in I am at the security gate." I really should have slept in like he did; I could have avoided my ridiculous attempt at gate climbing and be in the exact same position I was now.

"Adler speed skating arena media entrance. Get there now!" I replied.

I took off at a full sprint. Past the leaning barricades and the Ice

Palace and the parking lot. Past the smirking security guy. Past the craft services tent that was soon to be torn down and transported to some St. Petersburg county fair. Down the walkway next to the fence next to the road next to the other fence next to the open sewer in front of La Terrassa.

As I started to let up in speed—partly because I was approaching the media entrance to the speed skating palace but mainly because I was extremely out of shape—I saw a familiar face approaching.

"They *just* decided to start keeping people out of here without tickets today? Do they maybe want to warn people? Do they maybe want to have people enjoy the park on the last day of the Olympics?" Dan, like me—like a lot of us—was having a hard time wrapping his head around the Russian way of thinking.

"Let's just get those tickets and see the game," I said. I was too worked up about the possibility of missing the game to worry about logistics now.

Then my phone rang. It was Irena from Nike again.

"Jay, where are you?"

Oh, God, no.

"I'm right where we said to meet. At the entrance to the Adler media centre."

"I can't get through to there. The other side of the building is locked."

Oh, God, no.

"But I suppose I could meet you at the main security entrance."

The *very* entrance I was denied access to in the beginning.

At that moment I believe Elton John's "Circle of Life" from *The Lion King* soundtrack began playing in my head. I told Dan the good news and we wandered back, slowly, casually, to the main security entrance near the Bolshoy Ice Dome. There, we encountered a sea of faces—security, volunteers, broadcasters, and would-be spectators. I looked around and tried to spot our Nike contact, but I realized I had absolutely no idea what she looked like. I probably should have thought to ask what colour her hair was at the very least, but in my elated state I had completely forgotten. Then, out of the corner of my eye, I saw her. I don't know exactly how I knew it was her, I just did. Okay, maybe the head-to-toe Nike gear was a tipoff. She was carrying a purse and was standing with a young blond-haired fellow, presumably the contact she had met at USA Olympic House earlier. She saw me approaching, smiled, reached into her purse, and pulled out not one but two golden tickets.

"I am so sorry this was so difficult!" she said.

"Not difficult at all," I lied.

I thanked her and she was off—she wasn't even attending the game! Like so many other Russians, once their team lost the quarterfinal game to Finland they were no longer interested in the rest of the men's hockey results. I was reminded of another hockey-loving nation I once lived and worked in and am proud to be from—Canadians wouldn't be too interested in a gold-medal game without their home team playing either. Not that many differences between us when it's all said and done.

We walked past the very sweet and kind Russian volunteers with our valuable tickets in hand and strolled toward the Bolshoy Ice Dome. Underneath the dome was the entrance to the NHLPA players' lounge. We had spent plenty of time there over the course of our roughly three weeks in Sochi thanks to the fact that Dan's best friend happened to be former New York Islander crash 'n' banger and current PA employee Steve Webb. Early on during our tenure at La Terrassa, as we stayed up drinking until 6:00 a.m., Steve had surveyed the scene and dubbed it "the Frat House," a moniker that stuck for the remainder of the Games. Steve secured passes for Dan, me, and several others in our crew to hang out and relax in the PA lounge. This was no ordinary lounge. While not a huge space, the food they served was easily the best available within twenty miles of the Olympic Cauldron. Free beer and wine was available to all. Sure, the place was only supposed to be enjoyed by actual Olympic hockey players and their families, but we were willing to overlook that fact if they were.

At one point during the Games when I was hanging out in the lounge, I struck up a conversation with Latvian cult hero and former Carolina Hurricanes goaltender Arturs Irbe. *Irbe!* He always struck such a fascinating figure between the pipes with his diminutive stature and his bright white goalie pads and Jofa helmet with a cage. Irbe was working for the PA as a translator, seeing as he was fluent in Russian, but mostly he seemed to be just hanging out in the lounge. At one point during our conversation he explained to me how the game of hockey worked: "You need the coach, have to have the coach, then you need referees . . ." You can probably see where the conversation was headed. *Irbe!*

We met up with Peter Schrager at the PA lounge. He, like many of us, had just walked past the security guards at the gate to the lounge and they'd pretty much let it happen. Basically, the security was on par with your favourite nightclub. Sure, they were going to put you through the ringer the first couple of times you tried to get in, but after a while you became a harmless regular. Amazingly, Schrager hadn't been able to find someone to take his fourth ticket to the game, so it was just the three of us entering the Bolshoy that day for my second stab at hockey history.

Once again, the location of our seats proved that I am the luckiest and most undeserving man in the world. We wandered down the steps of the arena bowl, past the gold-medal-winning Canadian men's curling team, and took our seats—three rows behind Carey Price—to start the first period.

The result of the game was absolutely never in doubt. In all my years of watching Canadian international hockey, from the 1981 Canada Cup to the world junior powerhouses of the 1990s, Canada's performance in the 2014 gold-medal game was equal to almost all of it because of its simple, devastating precision. It was the way Canadian hockey is meant to be played—a real team coming together and playing their roles effectively even though the role players were the leading scorers on their respective NHL teams. It really warmed my heart to see how the Canadians were able to dominate a great hockey country like Sweden. The atmosphere in the arena paled in comparison to the gold-medal win on home soil in 2010, but it was still incredible to be sitting right behind Henrik Lundqvist as Sidney Crosby beat him on a breakaway. And it was also a blast to see the smiles on the faces of Canadian fans as we walked out of the Bolshoy Ice Dome to a concrete platform that overlooked the Dead Sea.

As the sun went down we snapped a few pictures with the Canadians who told us they missed us and asked us to return home from L.A. as soon as possible. We were excited to return to our new home in L.A. after almost three weeks on the road, but I had one more important stop to make first.

Chapter 20

The Sochi Sojourn,
Part 4: Moscow

Dan left Sochi right after the closing ceremonies. He changed his flight to leave early because he really missed his wife and kids. But like me, he was supposed to stay a few extra days in Russia. Our production manager, Celeste, had arranged for the entire crew to go on a tour of Moscow with a private guide. Moscow had never been at the top of my list of must-visit major world cities, but I figured since I was over there anyway it would be foolish not to go. So as soon as the last firework had gone off outside the Olympic Stadium, I began packing up my things for Russia's capital. But of course, not before bidding goodbye to Irina, Dasha, Igor, Toma, Anya, Kostya, and even the hotel's owner, Boris, who never seemed to wear anything but a Bosco Russian tracksuit. Boris didn't say a word to me the entire time I was there, but he was smiling proudly when we left, probably thrilled to be rid of us. It was a good thing we had literally rented the entire place or he may have had a few more complaints about us—other than just the ones that came from his staff.

Toma and Anya, the long-suffering waitresses who had been put on twenty-four-hour shifts throughout the Games, were in tears as we jumped into the Audi Q7s for one last ride to the airport. There was the usual talk of "You need to come visit us in the States!" and "You should all come work for us!" and "There are so many opportunities there!" but we all pretty much knew this was the last time we would see these wonderful people who had totally transformed my feelings about Russia and their citizens in such a positive way.

Shortly after returning to Los Angeles, we received word that most of the hotel staff had been laid off immediately after the Games. I wondered what happened to everyone who worked tirelessly in that hotel for those two hectic weeks. Most of them didn't live in Sochi, so they likely returned to their respective home towns and went on with their lives. But I like to think they look back on those few weeks fondly, and I hope the friendliness of our crew was a big part of the reason why.

Moscow turned out to be a very interesting trip to say the least. I wasn't fully prepared for what I was about to see and I certainly wasn't prepared for the traffic. When people ask me about living in Los Angeles and I tell them I love it, they usually say something like, "You love everything except the traffic, right?"

To which I reply, "The traffic in Los Angeles is like the traffic in Athabasca, Alberta, compared to Moscow."

We had arrived in February and the city was cold but still walkable, and that was a good thing because trying to take a cab anywhere was an exercise in extreme patience. The cab ride from the airport was an eye-opener—because of the traffic as well as the Communist-era apartment buildings that lined the freeway all the way to the core. If I had Vladimir Putin's ear, I might suggest that he stop picking fights with former Soviet states and instead put those rubles into Moscow's city infrastructure. There were entirely too few roads and entirely too many cars in that city. I had never experienced anything like it.

Once we were all secure in our hotel—a major upgrade from La Terrassa but still filled with the rich and pungent smell of cigarette smoke—we made arrangements for our guided tour of the city the next day. Then, we sat down for what was probably the first *real* meal any of us had eaten in weeks. Unfortunately, I can't remember where we ate, or what the meal consisted of, because as usual we were drinking vodka. Not in fancy cocktails but in shot glasses, icy cold with some sort of chaser on the side like a fruit juice. Sounds like a reasonable way to enjoy a good-quality bottle of Russian Beluga. Problem was, the servers in this quality establishment, like all quality Russian establishments, refused to let your shot glass go empty. Russians don't drink the entire shot, but rather sip it like a normal drink. And so, always doing our best to fit in, we followed suit. But the servers would literally be standing right behind us as we drank and ate away, so the second you took one sip of your vodka a dour gentleman would immediately appear behind you and fill that shot glass right up to the top again. Needless to say, this was a very dangerous way to drink vodka, and before we knew it, we were stumbling back to our hotel, completely lost and just praying we could remember which floor we were on so we could pass out in our comfy accommodations free of any dogs or cats that might already be sleeping in our beds.

The next day we met in the middle of Red Square for our guided tour by a lovely middle-aged Russian woman named Helena. She walked us all around the Square to the candy-cane coloured St. Basil Cathedral and then past the outside of the Kremlin, while Russian children and their families skated on the outdoor rink. The whole world should be lucky enough to visit Red Square someday and witness the incredible architecture—a true marvel of engineering and beauty. We continued back toward the main entrance of the square where Helena had arranged for us to leave our cameras with security near the gate so we could go see Lenin's Tomb. I had heard about Lenin's Tomb, but I suppose the reality of the thing had escaped me. The former Russian premier was literally embalmed and kept under glass so that the entire world would have an opportunity to see Russia's most important leader with their own eyes.

Surely this had to be a joke, right?

"The Russians tried traditional methods to preserve Lenin," said our guide Helena, as we prepared to head inside and down the stairs to the final resting place of the great leader, "but they didn't work. So the Russians developed their own way to preserve the body."

Sure they did! The Russians! How great is that? The process of actually keeping a body from breaking down completely didn't exist when Lenin died, so they came up with their own way of preserving him. And preserve him they did! Who could possibly question this?

We were led down a very dark set of stairs, past a gun-toting Russian military guard, around a corner past another gun-toting Russian military guard, to what appeared to be an altar that we had to climb a small set of stairs and pass two more gun-toting Russian military guards to reach. All of this was performed in single file, as if we were queuing for cafeteria food. As I climbed the stairs to the tomb, I could see him out of the corner of my eye. He looked like a Madame Tussauds replica of Vladimir Lenin, right down to the little beard. But he was the *real* thing. Evidently, the Russians had found a way to preserve him in a glass tomb for all these years.

I was highly confused by it all. Didn't the Russians find this just a little *weird*? Not to mention the fact that when I tried to stop for just a moment and take a closer look, another gun-toting Russian military guard barked at me in his mother tongue and told me to "keep moving" or perhaps to "not question our presidential embalming techniques and just go with it." I don't speak the language so it was difficult to be sure, but I certainly wasn't sticking around to ask for clarification. The whole exercise was over in about two minutes. We rounded the tomb, keeping a steady pace the entire way, and then climbed the stairs past two more gun-toting Russian military guards and finally emerged back into the light of day in Red Square. The experience stayed with me throughout the day—it was like a microcosm of Russia itself. You couldn't explain it and you weren't allowed to question it. You just had to go along with it. Just go along with *everything*.

As I boarded the plane back to L.A. the next day, I couldn't help but think that this may be the last time I was boarding a plane after covering an Olympic Games. And sure enough, just a few months after the Sochi Games had ended, NBC announced that they had reached an agreement with the IOC to continue broadcasting the Olympic Games in the U.S. until the year 2032. It was foolish to expect Fox to outbid NBC for broadcasting rights when they had already put a ton of money into securing the next two World Cups. And where was the first of those two World Cups taking place? Why, Russia, of course. The Sochi Olympic stadium had already been designated one of the 2018 World Cup venues. Was it possible that at least a few of us would end up back here in four years to cover an event that was arguably bigger than the Olympic Games because of our experience staying and working in the area? Was it possible we might all once again stay at La Terrassa? Perhaps by then the open sewer would have a lid on it. It would be a pretty sweet reunion, but the food would probably still be terrible.

When we returned to Los Angeles we were met with a lot of positive feedback for our humorous pieces from Sochi. In addition to our well-received tour of the Olympic venues—which we did outside the Olympic venues because of our lack of access to said venues—we also did several "one-part investigations" on hard-hitting issues that were affecting the Games: toilet quality, Olympic pin collecting, and of course stray dogs. A few veteran Fox directors told us that they were the funniest things they had ever seen broadcast out of the Fox Sports building, which may seem like a hollow compliment until you realize that Frank Caliendo and Rob Riggle have plied their comedic trade on the *NFL on Fox* studio show for a number of years. Others weren't so kind: "What the hell were you guys doing over there?" asked one production assistant bluntly. Covering the Olympics, we answered. That's what we do.

Chapter 21

Working with a Humble Comedy Legend

A few days after the launch of *Fox Sports Live* in August 2013, our entire crew gathered at the San Francisco Saloon on Pico Boulevard in Los Angeles for some post-show drinks and chit-chat. I sat at a table with three young production assistants, all about half my age, sipping beers and casually chatting about what had gone right so far (not much) and what had gone wrong (pretty much everything). At some point in the conversation, one of the guys, Oliver, who up to then hadn't said much, mentioned that he'd grown up in Los Angeles—in the Pacific Palisades neighbourhood, one of the nicest and most affluent areas of town—but that his dad was from Hamilton, Ontario.

Wow! I thought to myself. *Sounds like his parents have done pretty well for themselves down here. A real Canadian success story!*

I asked Oliver what his father did for a living. Unexpectedly, he looked down at his unfinished nachos and went silent.

Instantly, I felt bad, like I'd somehow crossed an invisible line. I had just met this kid and obviously I had absolutely no right to ask about his family's business.

"Just tell him," said Matt, one of the other young employees at the table.

Oliver stayed quiet.

"His dad is Martin Short," explained Matt.

Right. I guess "Canadian success story" was a bit of an understatement, then.

It's difficult to put into words exactly what the actor and comedian Martin Short means to me—to my entire family, really. We're *huge* fans. For the Onrait tribe, Martin Short is a Canadian national treasure.

We first encountered Martin and his incredible range of characters on *SCTV*. Later, we rooted for him when Hollywood beckoned with *¡Three Amigos!* and *Innerspace*. We hoped for a comeback with his sitcom *The Martin Short Show*, then hoped for another with his daytime talk show *The Martin Short Show*. We loved him as Franck the manic wedding planner in *Father of the Bride*, and we were brought to tears laughing at the "interviews" of bumbling Hollywood gossip-monger Jiminy Glick. We even saw him slay audiences with his one-man show *If I'd Saved, I Wouldn't Be Here*. But perhaps most of all, we lived for his appearances as a talk-show guest.

Back in the day, Martin Short appeared regularly as a guest on the *Late Show with David Letterman*, regaling audiences with hilarious stories about his family time at the cottage in Ontario, his road trips to Las Vegas with bandleader Paul Shaffer, and his encounters with the old Hollywood celebrities he loved and admired so much. If you were lucky, he'd even sing a song or two. Whatever he chose to do, Martin Short was as captivating a chat show guest as his generation had ever seen. Flipping on a talk show and finding out that Martin was one of the guests that evening was like winning a little personal entertainment lottery.

So when I discovered that his son worked for *Fox Sports Live*, I tried to play it cool, but I couldn't help but dream that someday he might be convinced to appear on our show.

Sure enough, following the release of his highly entertaining memoir *I Must Say: My Life as a Humble Comedy Legend* in the fall of 2014, Mr. Short agreed to appear as a guest on "The Jay and Dan Podcast" and *Fox Sports Live* to promote his book and new Fox sitcom, *Mulaney*. I tried to pretend the news didn't completely freak me out, but let's face it, I was a wreck.

When Martin arrived at the Fox studio he was accompanied by an assistant and wearing a bespoke black suit. He honestly looked twenty-five years younger than he actually was—without appearing to have undergone any cosmetic surgeries. Dan and I were blown away. The man could not have been more gracious and kind as we sat in the tiny audio booth where we record our podcast, discussing his career and laughing at the fact that one of our listeners had pointed out that my laugh sounded exactly like one of his SCTV characters, Bradley Allen, in a sketch called "Artisans and Their Art." The whole experience went swimmingly, and I was incredibly grateful and more than a little relieved because I had something else planned for him to do that afternoon that kept me distracted throughout the interview. And to be honest, despite Martin's reputation for being a good sport, I wasn't entirely sure how he'd react to my idea.

I had written a sketch for Martin to appear in on our show. Can you imagine the balls I had even thinking to do something like that? This was a man who *pioneered* the art of sketch comedy on *SCTV*— which I still consider to be the greatest show to come out of Canada . . . *ever*. He then went on to save *Saturday Night Live*, appearing in the famous all-star cast alongside other comedy heavyweights like Billy Crystal and Christopher Guest. The guy was born to be a sketch comedian. I, on the other hand, was definitely not. Still, I couldn't pass up the opportunity to write something under the small hope that he might actually consider performing it.

Thankfully, Martin's gracious nature shone through that day, and after listening to us pitch a small "walk-on" for the show, he agreed to participate in the sketch. We finished up the podcast interview, then walked the few steps to Studio B with Martin's assistant and a bunch of other Fox PR people in tow. Dan and I got set up behind our desk and explained the premise to Martin. I handed him a copy of my two-page comedic opus, and he went off to a corner to read it over. About two minutes later he returned ready to go. *Two minutes!* That couldn't possibly be enough time to absorb all the genius lines I'd written for him, could it?

It was. We did two takes. The first one was pretty much perfect, but we all agreed another would be a good idea just for safety. The sketch went something like this:

JAY: Before we get to "The 1," our top play of the day . . .
[Martin Short suddenly appears out of nowhere.]
DAN: Martin Short? What are *you* doing here?
MARTIN: Well, I was just, uh, looking for my son Oliver. He works on this show and I was just . . . [Martin looks around] You call this a show, right?

JAY: Oh yeah! I gotta say, Oliver is doing a terrific job, by the way.

MARTIN: Oh, thank you. Although he tells me you guys call him Alan.

DAN: Alan's . . . short for Oliver in our world, so . . .

JAY [interrupting]: Hey, congratulations on getting your face on a Canadian stamp! That is quite an honour, sir.

MARTIN: Yeah, well . . . you know . . .

JAY [sheepishly]: Mr. Short, do you think maybe we might get our faces on a Canadian stamp one day?

MARTIN [laughing]: Oh, no. No, no, no. Don't hold your breath on that one. You see, because getting your face on a Canadian stamp is something reserved for real Canadian celebrities. Jim Carrey. Catherine O'Hara. And of course, myself. I mean, if they put you two on a stamp, who's next? Pierre Trudeau?

DAN: Well, he was the prime minister of Canada.

MARTIN: Exactly . . . Well, I've got to return now. We're presently shooting my new show *Mulaney*, which airs on Fox every Sunday.

DAN: Wow! You're filming the show right now?

MARTIN: Yeah. Well, actually no. But I'm Canadian. We're too polite to just walk away. I can't say "I'm bored. This has been really bad. Neither one of you flosses." I'm not going to say that.

JAY: Right.

MARTIN: But Jan, Dean, it is such a thrill to see you guys. And really, just keep it up because . . . someone's gonna watch.

JAY: Yeah, someday.

DAN: We hope so.

MARTIN: Anyway, break a leg.

[Martin Short exits.]

JAY: Thank you very much, Mr. Short. What a terrific person!

DAN: Yeah.
JAY: He seemed nice.
And . . . *scene.*

He really was. He was really a terrific guy. He bid us all goodbye, snapped a few pictures with the crew, and just as quickly as he'd arrived, he was gone. Heading back home to the Pacific Palisades.

How does one judge success in the entertainment industry in this day and age? Or more accurately, how does a guy like me—who decided to leave a comfy and successful situation in Canada for a terrifying and unsure one in the United States— judge success?

Ratings? Yeah, that's definitely part of it. Money? That is undeniably a factor. Happiness? I'm not sure most people know what that means.

But the second Martin Short started reading and performing words that I'd written, I sat back and realized that this was as good a measuring stick for success as I was likely to ever find. Having someone you admire so much not only turn out to be a terrific person but also grant you a huge favour when he really had no reason to . . . it's sort of inspiring! Maybe I'm just getting older and more reflective. Or maybe I just can't believe how nice someone like Martin Short could be to a couple of relative nobodies after years and years of success. But if it all ended tomorrow and Fox decided not to renew our contracts and the U.S. Customs and Immigration people showed up at our doors with strict instructions to leave the country immediately or be jailed, I would be happy knowing that I got to perform—*on television*—with one of my greatest comedy heroes.

Sure, I would probably be a tad upset about the jail part, but this is Martin Short we're talking about here—the jail part would be worth it.

Chapter 22

Saskatchewan

A few years ago, I was in Regina to speak at a fundraising dinner for the University of Regina Rams. It was a wonderful time. Afterwards, a bunch of people on the organizing committee took me out, and we had a bit of a late night. I ended up crashing around 4:30 a.m. Unfortunately, I had a 9:00 a.m. flight. I dragged myself out of bed a few hours later and hopped into my rental car to drive to the airport. I don't drive in Regina much, so someone drew me a map on a napkin at Earl's the night before. It was a surprisingly good map considering it was drawn by a drunk.

So I got on the road, and I was doing pretty well considering I was fifty percent asleep and one hundred percent hungover, but then I realized I'd missed a turn. I'd have to turn around and go back. So, I pulled off the main road onto a residential street, and I made what seemed to me like a simple U-turn. Unfortunately, I took it just a bit too wide and managed to drive right into a pile of

241

snow that had been pushed up on the curb. No problem. I thought. I was in an SUV, after all. So I threw that bad boy into reverse and prepared to rip out of there. But I didn't move. The wheels spun and spun. I was stuck. At 7:30 a.m. on a Sunday morning in the middle of a deserted residential street in Regina. With absolutely no one around to help me push.

To sum up: I had managed to get the rental car stuck and my flight was leaving in an hour and a half. The Regina transit system leaves much to be desired, and getting a cab that early on a Sunday in Regina was going to be a bit of a stretch.

I tried not to panic. I got out of the SUV, walked back to the main road, and at that very moment, a police car drove by. I waved it down. He pulled over with a look on his face that said, "This guy must be from Ontario."

I told the officer I had gotten my rental car stuck in the snow, and now he gave me a look that said: "No, this guy isn't from Ontario. Judging by the way he drives, he clearly grew up in Alberta."

I asked him if there was any possible way he might consider giving me a ride to the airport—because I knew all the flights back to Toronto would be booked solid by Ontario politicians who had flown out to Saskatchewan to beg for money.

"If I drive you to the airport, what are you going to do with the rental car?" he asked.

"I'm . . . going to leave it here," I said.

The cop thought about that for a second and said, "Okay, I'll drive you to the airport, but only because your network shows Rider games."

Finally, my D-list celebrity status had gotten me out of a jam.

I happily jumped into the back of the cop car—the "cage" if you will—and tried to look menacing as I peered out the window. I imagined that I was a famous bank robber, and I had finally been caught after cleaning out vaults across the prairies. "The Bad Driving Bandit," they'd call me.

Soon, we arrived at the airport and I bid the cop goodbye, promising him that I would send someone out for the rental car. I immediately walked up to the Enterprise Rent-A-Car stand and was greeted by a nice young man named Andy.

"Hi, Andy," I said.

"Oh, hello, Mr. Onrait," said Andy cheerfully. "How was the car?"

"Well, Andy . . . it *was* good. It *was* very good. Unfortunately, at this very moment, it's not good at all. Because it's not moving."

"Oh, no," said Andy in a tone that didn't give away anything, even if he had suddenly come to the (correct) conclusion that renting a car to me had been a horrible, horrible mistake.

"Yes, Andy, as it turns out, I am not a very good driver. I managed to drive your beautiful, shiny rental car into a snowbank. Not even a snowbank, really, probably a small pile of snow that an old lady pushed off her driveway. Nevertheless, I am here, but the truck is not."

"You left it there?" asked Andy.

"I'm afraid I did," I replied sheepishly.

For a split second I imagined how embarrassing this was about to become once Andy realized what I'd done. Surely Andy would fly into a rage, shouting and swearing at me in the middle of the airport while sleepy-eyed passengers stared with mouths agape. I grimaced and waited for my reprimand. Andy spoke:

"Don't worry about it!"

"I'm sorry?"

"Happens all the time! Oh, yeah, people are always getting these things stuck. I'm sure it's fine."

"But it's stuck in the middle of a residential neighbourhood. It's just sitting there. And now that I stop to think about it, I'm pretty sure the door is unlocked!"

Andy didn't even skip a beat. "People are friendly in this town. It'll be fine there. It's probably safer there than in the airport parking lot! I'll just call a couple of guys right now and send them over to pick it up."

"You're going to call a couple of guys at eight in the morning? On a Sunday? I don't think they're going to like that call."

"They're used to it," explained Andy. "Remember what I said, Jay? This happens *all* the time!" After some more feeble protesting, I handed Andy the keys and got on my way.

As it turns out, this kind of thing *does not* happen all the time. The two guys that Andy called had to return to the car *three* times, each time with bigger shovels, before they managed to get it free. I feel pretty bad about that, but I sent them some Rider tickets, so I figure that means we're more or less even.

On another trip to Saskatchewan, when my dad and I were visiting my eighty-nine-year-old grandfather in Balcarres, my father's hometown, we were met at the Regina airport by his "driver" and longtime best buddy, Ivan (who is comparably youthful at just seventy-five years old). So there's me, my dad, Grandpa, and Ivan, all piled into Ivan's minivan for the drive to Balcarres, and my grandfather asked me if we would be interested in making a stop at the Balgonie Hotel Bar. And let me tell you, when someone asks if you want to stop at the Balgonie Hotel Bar, just say yes. Don't ask questions.

Balgonie is a town of about 600 people, and the bar is fairly easy to find. As we pulled into the lot, I made to get out of the van, but Grandpa stopped me, saying, "Stay here. I'll go in." I quickly realized that this wasn't your regular bar stop—this was a stop to pick up beer that we would then proceed to drink on the drive back to my grandfather's house. Now, I want to make it clear that I definitely do not condone drinking and driving, but when your eighty-nine-year-old grandfather decides he wants to share a case of road beers with you on the drive home, it's best to play it cool, start cracking open those bottles, and try to make sure the driver keeps it between the lines.

About two years later, Dan and I were hosting a "Jay and Dan Podcast" and commenting on the fact that comedian Brent Butt had recently announced that the cast of his hit Canadian sitcom *Corner Gas* was reuniting to make a movie. I always loved the show because it was funny and I completely understood the world in which it existed. The fictional small Saskatchewan town of Dog River could have been any small Saskatchewan town, including my parents' home town of Balcarres. That's why people from Saskatchewan loved the show so much. If anyone other than Brent, himself a native of Tisdale, Saskatchewan, had tried to write and produce the show, there would have been cries of inauthenticity, but like all great writers, Brent was simply writing about what he knew. This was the life he probably would have led had he never left Tisdale, population 2,000.

When Twitter blew up with the news that the cast of *Corner Gas* was reuniting, we were excited about it and happy for Brent. As I mentioned in *Anchorboy*, just when things were at their worst for my show *The Week That Was*, Brent stepped up and helped me by contributing his voice for a sketch we had hastily put together, free of charge. I never forgot how gracious he was with his time and talent. So when Brent and his producers announced the *Corner Gas* movie, I thought it was appropriate that we got the word out to our podcast listeners, most of whom are Canadian after all.

But being the fame whores we are, Dan and I refused to simply leave it at that. We also implored our podcast listeners to tweet at Brent, encouraging him to actually put us in the movie as extras. "We could be sitting in the background drinking Pilsner beer at the town bar," we said, "or drinking Vico at the Ruby." When I explain Vico to people outside of the province, I usually tell them it's what Saskatchewanites of a certain age call chocolate milk. As my parents explained it to me, Vico was a brand of chocolate milk that was available in the province when they grew up—the only brand, apparently, as years went by before anyone in the 306 area code referred to chocolate milk as anything else but Vico. It even appeared on most restaurant menus in the province, confusing the hell out of tourists.

We didn't give the whole thing much thought after the podcast was over, but lo and behold the power of the "Jay and Dan Podcast" fan is a wonderful thing. The producers of the movie, and Brent himself, were suddenly aware of the little shitstorm we were causing. About three days after the podcast aired I felt bad about bugging Brent and sent him a direct message:

"Apologies for our obnoxiousness but we are genuinely thrilled for all your success. Love the fact that you're doing a *Corner Gas* film . . . And would genuinely love to be associated with it in any way possible."

Brent wrote back a few hours later: "We'd love to have you guys! Not sure doing what, but SOMETHING dammit! I've already had a chat with production about it. Talk next week."

I figured this meant we would inevitably get our wish and be extras in the background of a scene. I couldn't wait. But Brent surprised me with something better. A week later an email arrived in my inbox, saying: "I have written you each a line in the movie."

This was followed by an email from the film's executive producer,

Virginia Thompson: "We are thrilled to have you in the movie. We will fly you up on Sunday, June 29th, and film your scene on Monday, June 30th, then fly you back to L.A. on Tuesday, July 1st."

Back to L.A. on Canada Day—how appropriate.

And so on Sunday, June 29th, I dragged myself out of bed at 4:30 a.m. and drove to LAX to catch a flight to Minneapolis. There we connected on a flight to Regina, and after a few twists and turns that included running into Wawota, Saskatchewan native and Washington Capitals forward Brooks Laich—which resulted in us nearly missing our connecting flight—we eventually made it to a rainy, soggy Regina where we were supposed to be Brent's guests at the Saskatchewan Roughriders CFL home opener against Hamilton.

The rain was Biblically bad that day, literally flooding the streets of the city, and like the pampered Hollywood denizens we are, the team quickly moved the cast of the movie—including me and Dan and our former TSN cohort Darren Dutchyshen, who was also in the film—into the Pilsner Place, an enclosed bar and viewing area where we stayed warm and dry while the poor diehards got soaked in the stands outside. *Sports Illustrated* senior football writer Peter King was at the game as part of a week-long series he was writing about the Canadian Football League, and I felt bad that he wasn't getting the "proper" Roughriders game experience. Later, King told our mutual friend Peter Schrager that he received multiple tweets the following day from Roughrider fans apologizing for the bad weather that had occurred—so Canadian to apologize for bad weather they had absolutely no control over.

The next day my uncle Kim—my dad's brother—and my cousin Morgan picked me up at the Hotel Saskatchewan at 8:00 a.m. I was still a little groggy from the night before—am I ever not groggy from the night before? (*Groggy from the Night Before* was an alternate title for this book.) We had ventured out to popular Regina pub O'Hanlon's, and one of our old friends from the Kraft Celebration Tour, Tracy Westgard, had shown up to pour the tequila. Nonetheless, we braved the soggy weather for the drive northeast to Balcarres to visit my grandfather, now ninety-one years old and living in a seniors' home. Past Balgonie, where we had stopped at the bar; past Fort Qu'Appelle, where we used to get Kentucky Fried Chicken; past the Mission Ridge Winter Park on Katepwa Lake, where Olympic bronze medallist Mark McMorris and his brother Craig first learned to snowboard on one of the smallest "ski hills" imaginable; past power line after power line and soggy field after soggy field; past old combines lined up in a row like sculptures; and past brand-new metal grain elevators that didn't have half the personality of the old, worn-down, sun-damaged wooden ones, until finally we reached the outskirts of Balcarres. It was here that my parents had grown up and my great grandfather, Gaston Onrait, had arrived from France over one hundred years before to claim his plot of land like every other immigrant who dreamed of the vast space and opportunities this young country offered. Gaston and his young bride, Emerence, weren't the world's greatest farmers, but they raised nine children on that farm and made a life for themselves in their new country. For years, Balcarres was a thriving prairie town with a booming agriculture industry and a bustling main street—it even had a movie theatre. Now it resembles the fictional town that Brent created in *Corner Gas*. Most of the stores on Main Street have closed up, and although there's still a hospital, still a drugstore, and still a school, frankly the only thing keeping the school open is the neighbouring First Nations reserves.

We drove past the Balcarres Hotel and Bar. In recent years I had spent many a night there while visiting Grandpa, and now the current owners had put it up for sale, asking an astonishing $300,000 for the place. "I wouldn't give them $300," said my uncle, who had also grown up in this town and had since moved on to a life in the city.

We pulled up to the Balcarres Integrated Care Centre, nestled in between the school and the hospital, and just down the street from the home of Ervin Baber, a man who'd been hugely influential on my father, as he had owned the local drugstore in town, employed him as a teenager, and even loaned him some money so he could attend pharmacy school. We got out of the car and walked past the rain-soaked ditch along the gravel road, making our way up the walkway to the front door. In the entranceway four seniors gathered, chatting and killing time until lunch, while the building's resident dog lounged at their feet. They all stared at me like I was a ghost, a feeling I was used to from delivering prescriptions to the Athabasca Seniors Homes during my teenage years in high school. Every person who entered was someone to break the monotony of living there, and they never got used to seeing my face—they would always stare.

Down the hallway we walked, after saying hello to Ayda, my grandfather's most recent girlfriend. After my grandmother passed in 1986, he quickly took up with Tish "the Dish" Garden, and she became for all intents and purposes a surrogate grandmother to us until her death in 2012. Now Ayda was in the picture. We found Grandpa's room and my uncle and cousin opened the door. I was last to enter, and upon my arrival my grandfather said the words I had heard him say so many times when I surprised him with visits over the years.

"Oh, for God's sake, what the bloody hell are you doing here?" with a grin the size of Saskatchewan itself.

The weather outside wasn't even that cold, but Grandpa had a heater blasting and the whole room felt like a steam bath. The television set was cranked to a level that would have made most people's ears bleed. He had been watching *Live with Kelly and Michael*, and my uncle later explained that usually when he and Ayda watched television together the sound was cranked to unbelievable volumes because neither of them could hear a thing. Ayda later joined us in the room, and I caught Grandpa up on the reason I had come to Saskatchewan in the first place. He was a fan of *Corner Gas*, and I really hoped he would be able to see the movie on television that fall.

He talked for a while about the building's caretaker, Jimmy Pigeon, who fixed things around the facility but had somehow become a bee in his bonnet. Grandpa was in decent health and of sharp mind, but he could barely walk anymore, and he couldn't lift his arms much higher than to turn up the volume on the remote— the result of years spent sanding down the exteriors of cars in his autobody shop. I joked that my Chinese wife and I were going to buy the old café on Main Street that had now been shut down for two years and launch a Chinese food restaurant there, but he informed me that two Chinese families had already moved to town and done the same thing in other buildings. That town may not have had much, but at least it had a couple of different Cantonese takeout options.

After about an hour we had to leave as I was due on set to film my one-line part in the movie with Dan and Darren. Grandpa reached for his walker, pulled himself up, and began the slow plod for the front door to see us out. He used a rolling walker now and basically leaned on it, his legs and hips were just not going to cut it anymore. But he still seemed healthy and happy for a guy who had outlived all of those nine other brothers and sisters to be ninety-one. I noticed his shirt was untucked and hanging out the back of his jeans, which were probably now three sizes too big for him, as he was about as skinny as I was at fourteen. As he reached the doorway to his room,

Ayda saw the shirt and quickly tucked it into the back of his pants in an exceptionally sweet moment that nearly made me well up on the spot.

Shirt secure, Grandpa then rolled down the hallway—slowly but steadily—to the front door where the four guys were still sitting and chatting while the dog slumbered beneath their feet.

We bid him goodbye, and as we walked out the front entrance I heard him say to the other guys in the doorway with a laugh: "There goes my little grandson."

Acknowledgements

Even though the entire book is dedicated to her, no acknowledgements would be complete without mentioning my beautiful wife, Chobi, who endured many afternoons of my wandering off to the Refinery Coffee House in Santa Monica and missing out on quality time together. To make matters worse, much of the last stages of book writing happened while she was pregnant with our first child. Once again she made the sacrifices necessary for me to be able to work on my "art." (I put that last sentence in so that she could laugh at it over and over.) She also took the time to read the book before it was published and, despite finding it a bit "crass," offered many wonderful suggestions for making it better. I can't even begin to express the love I have for this woman. She truly makes life worth living. Every day with her gets better and better.

Another heartfelt thank you goes out to my editor and good friend, Doug Richmond, who worked tirelessly on this book and took the time to meet up with me on early mornings when he was probably hungover from the night before because he is a wild man about town. Doug put so much effort into this book, and I truly believe it's better than the last one in large part because of all the work Doug put into it. Thanks, buddy, and let's grab a few pints at Ronnie's soon.

Also huge thanks to everyone at HarperCollins who worked tirelessly to get this epic to print: Patricia MacDonald, Erin Parker, Greg Tabor, Kelly Hope, Jason Pratt and ketchup chip enthusiast Kelsey Marshall. You guys are amazing and I look forward to working with you on the third book, about my wife and I having American-born children so we can't get kicked out of the States. Tentative title: *Anchorbaby.*

My literary agent, Carly Watters, is the number one reason I can now say I have two published books on bookshelves across North America. She was the one who spearheaded *Anchorboy*, and she was the one who encouraged me to get to work right away on a second book even if I was somewhat unsure about my ability to get the work done. Carly never stopped believing that I could finish another one, and along the way she offered wonderful advice and encouragement about the text. She's not just an agent but a great friend in my life.

Thanks to my best friend, Peter Sayn-Wittgenstein, for reading an early draft of this book and offering some great advice.

I can't say enough how lucky I am to have such close friends from my days growing up and living in the Canadian prairies and living and working across Canada and now the United States. You have not only helped to provide content for me to write about, you have always been there for me when I needed you. Work colleagues from Saskatoon to Winnipeg to Toronto to Los Angeles form my social circle and provide me with so much joy on a day-to-day basis throughout my career. Except Producer Tim. He's a real dick. Just kidding, Producer Tim! You're the best.

Special thanks to my mother and father, who probably have mixed feelings about at least 42 percent of the content in this book. They have never been less than exceptional about pushing me to try to step outside my comfort zone and do work like this that doesn't fall under my "regular work." My dad always wanted me to write books, but he was probably not counting on being such a prominently featured subject in them. Thanks, Mom and Dad, for not only raising me but also being good sports and not demanding royalties. Lots of love to my mother-in-law, Patty, and brother- and sister-in-law, Todd and Natalya. Special thanks to my sister, Erin, and her family: my brother-in-law Trevor, nephews Noah and Keaton, and niece Brooklyn, who threw me a pretty awesome Little Mermaid–themed birthday party last year. None of you kids will be able to read this book until you are twenty-five or so.

My good friend and broadcast colleague Dan O'Toole continues to be an endless source of entertainment each and every night on the set of *Fox Sports Live* and when he's trying to figure out how to avoid spending money on a cell phone. Thanks for taking care of all the logistics of our newly launched website, JayandDan.com, while I was busy putting the finishing touches on this future Giller Prize winner.

Huge thanks to my bosses at Fox Sports including Eric Shanks, John Entz, Jacob Ullman, David Nathanson, Michael Hughes, Jamie Horowitz, and everyone who works tirelessly with us every day to put together what I happen to think is a pretty watchable hour of television. No small feat in this day and age. Here's hoping for many more wonderful years together enjoying Boston Market catering.

Big thanks to Peter Schrager, my friend and colleague at Fox Sports, for writing a foreword for this book that was downright hilarious. If you get a chance, you should check out some of the books that Pete has written: *Out of the Blue* with Victor Cruz and *Strength of a Champion* with O.J. Brigance. The guy can really write!

Acknowledgements

Thanks to my grandpa for showing me how to be a real man despite my not quite achieving that goal.

Finally, thanks to everyone in Canada who keeps asking us to come back. We will, someday.